"I pledge to be active this summer,
to be kind to myself, and to others."

_____
Name

20___
Year

Let's Get Ready for Sixth Grade!

Summer Fit Fifth to Sixth Grade

Author: Dr. Leland Graham

Consulting Editor: Jennifer Moore, Teacher at Evansdale Elementary, Dekalb Schools, Atlanta, GA

Fitness and Nutrition: Lisa Roberts RN, BSN, PHN, James Cordova, Charles Miller, Steve Edwards, Missy Jones, Barbara Sherwood, John Bartlette, Malu Egido, Michael Ward

Healthy Family Lifestyle: Jay and Jen Jacobs & Marci and Courtney Crozier

Layout and Design: Scott Aucutt

Cover Design and Illustrations: Andy Carlson

Illustrations: Roxanne Ottley and Scott Aucutt

Series Created by George Starks

Summer Fit Dedication

Summer Fit is dedicated to Julia Hobbs and Carla Fisher who are the authors and unsung heroes of the original summer workbook series that helped establish the importance of summer learning. These women helped pioneer summer learning and dedicated their lives to teaching children and supporting parents. Carla and Julia made the world a better place by touching the lives of others using their love of education.

Summer Fit is also dedicated to Michael Starks whose presence is missed dearly, but who continues to teach us every day the importance of having courage in difficult times and treating others with respect, dignity, and a genuine concern for others.

Summer Fit Caution

If you have any questions regarding your child's ability to complete any of the suggested fitness activities consult your family doctor or child's pediatrician. Some of these exercises may require adult supervision. Children should stretch and warm up before exercises. Do not push children past their comfort level or ability. These physical fitness activities were created to be fun for parents and caregivers as well as the child, but not as a professional training or weight loss program. Exercise should stop immediately if you or your child experiences any of the following symptoms: pain, feeling dizzy or faint, nausea, or severe fatigue.

Summer Fit Copyright

Special thanks to the Terry Fox Foundation for use of Terry's photo and inspiring us all to contribute to making the world a better place for others each in our own way.

Printed in the USA
All Rights Reserved
ISBN: 978-0-9853526-2-2
www.SummerFitLearning.com

TABLE OF CONTENTS

Parent Section

Activities and Exercises

Extras

Dear Parents,

Without opportunities to learn and practice essential skills over the summer months, most children fall behind academically. Research shows that summer learning loss varies, but that children can lose the equivalency of 2.5 months of math and 2 months of reading skills while away from school. In addition, children lose more than just academic knowledge during the summer. Research also shows that children are at greater risk of actually gaining more weight during summer vacation than during the school year:

All young people experience learning losses when they do not engage in educational activities during the summer. Research spanning 100 years shows that students typically score lower on standardized tests at the end of summer vacation than they do on the same tests at the beginning of the summer (White, 1906; Heyns, 1978; Entwisle & Alexander 1992; Cooper, 1996; Downey et al, 2004).

Research shows that children gain weight three times faster during the summer months – gaining as much weight during the summer as they do during the entire school year – even though the summertime is three times shorter. Von Hippel, P. T., Powell, B., Downey, D.B., & Rowland, N. (2007).

In the New York City school system, elementary and middle school students who placed in the top third of a fitness scale had better math and reading scores than students in the bottom third of the fitness scale. Those who were in the top 5% for fitness scored an average of 36 percentage points higher on state reading and math exams than did the least-fit 5%. New York City Department of Health. (2009)

Summer vacation is a great opportunity to use a variety of resources and programs to extend the academic learning experience and to reinforce life and social skills. It is an opportunity to give learning a different look and feel than what children are used to during the school year. Summer is a season that should be fun and carefree, but do not underestimate the opportunity and importance of helping children prepare for the upcoming school year. The key to a successful new school year is keeping your children active and learning this summer!

Sincerely,

Summer Fit Learning

FACT
You are your
child's greatest
teacher.

Purpose

The purpose of Summer Fit is to offer a comprehensive program for parents that promotes health and physical activity along side of academic and social skills. Summer Fit is designed to help create healthy and balanced family lifestyles.

Stay Smart

Summer Fit contains activities in reading, writing, math, language arts, science, and geography.

Program Components

Summer Fit activities and exercises are divided into 10 sections to correlate with the traditional 10 weeks of summer. Each section begins with a weekly overview and incentive calendar so parents and children can talk about the week ahead while reviewing the previous week. There are 10 pages of activities for each week. The child does 2 pages a day that should take 20-30 minutes a day to complete. Each day offers a simple routine to reinforce basic skills and includes a physical fitness exercise and healthy habit. Each week also reinforces a core value on a daily basis to build character and social skills. Activities start off easy and progressively get more difficult so by the end of the workbook children are mentally, physically and socially prepared for the grade ahead.

Stay Cool

Summer Fit uses core value activities and role models to reinforce the importance of good character and social skills.

Stay Active

Summer Fit uses a daily fitness exercise and wellness tips to keep children moving and having fun.

Summer Fit includes a daily exercise program that children complete as part of their one-page of activities a day. These daily exercises and movement activities foster active lifestyles and get parents and children moving together.

Summer Fit uses daily value-based activities to reinforce good behavior.

Summer Fit promotes the body-brain connection and gives parents the tools to motivate children to use both.

Summer Fit includes an online component that gives children and parents additional summer learning and fitness resources at SummerFitLearning.com.

Summer Fit contains activities and exercises created by educators, parents and trainers committed to creating active learning environments that include movement and play as part of the learning experience.

Summer Fit uses role models from around the world to introduce and reinforce core values and the importance of good behavior.

Teaching the Whole Child

The Whole Child philosophy is based on the belief that every child should be healthy, engaged, supported and challenged in all aspects of their lives. Investing in the *overall* development of your child is critical to their personal health and well being. There is increased awareness that a balanced approach to nurturing and teaching our children will benefit all aspects of their lives; therefore creating well rounded students who are better equipped to successfully navigate the ups and downs of their education careers.

Supports Common Core Standards

The Common Core provides teachers and parents with a common understanding of what students are expected to learn. These standards will provide appropriate benchmarks for all students, regardless of where they live and be applied for students in grades K-12. Summer Fit is aligned to Common Core Standards.

Learn more at: CoreStandards.org

Top 5 Parent Summer Tips

1 Routine: Set a time and a place for your child to complete their activities and exercises each day.

2 Balance: Use a combination of resources to reinforce basic skills in fun ways. Integrate technology with traditional learning, but do not replace one with another.

3 Motivate and Encourage: Inspire your child to complete their daily activities and exercises. Get excited and show your support of their accomplishments!

4 Play as a Family: Slap "high 5," jump up and down and get silly! Show how fun it is to be active by doing it yourself! Health Experts recommend 60 minutes of play a day and kids love seeing parents playing and having fun!

5 Eat Healthy (and together): Kids are more likely to eat less healthy during the summer, than during the school year. Put food back on the table and eat together at least once a day.

Health and Wellness in the Home

Physical activity is critical to your child's health and well-being. Research shows that children with better health are in school more days, learn better, have higher self esteem and lower risk of developing chronic diseases.

Exercise Provides:

✔ Stronger muscles and bones

✔ Leaner body because exercise helps control body fat

✔ Increased blood flow to the brain and wellness at home

✔ Lower blood pressure and blood cholesterol levels

✔ Kids who are active are less likely to develop weight issues, display more self-confidence, perform better academically and enjoy a better overall quality of life!

Tips from a former *Biggest Loser*

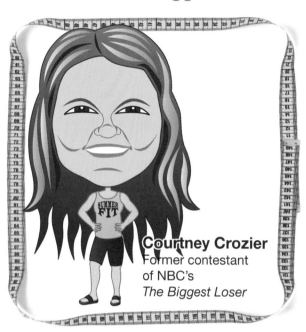

Courtney Crozier
Former contestant of NBC's *The Biggest Loser*

Courtney Crozier lost 110 pounds on Season 11 of NBC's *The Biggest Loser*.

Sedentary lifestyles, weight issues and unhealthy habits need to be addressed at home. It is more likely that your child will include healthy habits as part of their everyday life if they understand:

✔ Why staying active and eating healthy is important

✔ What are healthy habits and what are not

✔ How to be healthy, active and happy

Go to the Health and Wellness Index in the back of the book for more Family Health and Wellness Tips.

Warm Up!

It is always best to prepare your body for any physical activity by moving around and stretching.

Get Loose! Stretch!

Move your head from side to side, trying to touch each shoulder. Now move your head forward, touching your chin to your chest and then looking up and back as far as you can, trying to touch your back with the back of your head.

Touch your toes when standing, bend over at the waist and touch the end of your toes or the floor. Hold this for 10 seconds.

Get Moving

Walk or jog for 3-5 minutes to warm up before you exercise. Shake your arms and roll your shoulders when you are finished walking or jogging.

Healthy Eating and Nutrition

A healthy diet and daily exercise will maximize the likelihood of children growing up healthy and strong. Children are still growing and adding bone mass, so a balanced diet is very important to their overall health. Provide three nutritious meals a day that include fruits and vegetables. Try to limit fast food consumption, and find time to cook more at home where you know the source of your food and how your food is prepared. Provide your child with healthy, well-portioned snacks, and try to keep them from eating too much at a time.

SCORE! A HEALTHY EATING GOAL

As a rule of thumb, avoid foods and drinks that are high in sugars, fat, or caffeine. Try to provide fruits, vegetables, grains, lean meats, chicken, fish, and low-fat dairy products as part of a healthy meal when possible. Obesity and being overweight, even in children, can significantly increase the risk of heart disease, diabetes, and other chronic illnesses. Creating an active lifestyle this summer that includes healthy eating and exercise will help your child maintain a healthy weight and protect them from certain illnesses throughout the year.

Let's Eat Healthy!

5 Steps to Improve Eating Habits of Your Family

1) Make fresh fruits and veggies readily available.
2) Cook more at home, and sit down for dinner as a family.
3) Limit consumption of soda, desserts and sugary cereals.
4) Serve smaller portions.
5) Limit snacks to just one or two daily.

Technology and Child Development

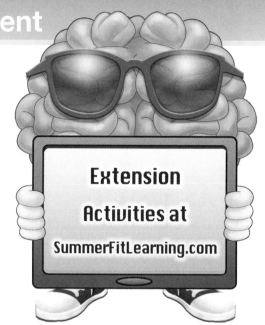

Children start developing initiative and creativity at a young age. Technology offers children additional outlets to learn and demonstrate their creativity. However, it is critical that active playtime and traditional learning resources included as an essential part of the child's daily routine in addition to technology use. Used appropriately, computers can be a positive element of children's play and learning as they explore and experiment. Screen time (including TV, computer, phone and games) should be limited to a maximum of one to two hours per day for young children (American Academy of Pediatrics). High Screen time is associated with a more sedentary lifestyle and excess snacking.

Extension Activities at SummerFitLearning.com

3 KEYS TO TECH SUCCESS

1 Consider technology as one tool among many used to enhance learning, not as a replacement for child interactions with each other, with adults, or other modes of learning.

2 Explore touch screens with a wide variety of appropriate interactive media experiences with your child. Verbally communicate with them the concepts of the game or apps that engage them. Express interest and encouragement of their performance.

3 Establish "No Screen Zones" for children such as the dinner table at home and in public settings. Screens create barriers that are difficult to talk through and can easily isolate children and parents. Establishing appropriate times and places to use technology will help children develop "tech-etiquette."

Core Values in the Home

Understanding core values allows your child to have a clearer understanding of their own behavior in your home, in their classroom and in our communities. Core values are fundamental to society and are incorporated into our civil laws, but are taught first and foremost at home. Parents and guardians are the most important and influential people in a child's life. It is up to you to raise children who respect and accept themselves, and others around them.

Role Models

A role model is a person who serves as an example of a particular value or trait. There are many people today, and throughout history, who exemplify in their own actions the values that we strive to have ourselves, and teach our children.

Mother Teresa
Winner of the Nobel Prize

Rosa Parks
Advocate for civil rights

Bullying

In recent years, bullying has become a leading topic of concern. It is a complex issue, and can be difficult for parents to know what to do when they hear that their child is being bullied or is bullying others. Bullying is always wrong. It is critical that you intervene appropriately when bullying occurs. Make sure your child understands what bullying means. Check in with your child often to make sure he/she knows you are interested and aware of what is going on in their social lives.

Learn more at StopBullying.gov

Bethany Hamilton
Lost her arm in a shark attack while surfing and continues to surf.

Books Build Better Brains!

Reading is considered the gateway to all learning, so it is critical as a parent or caregiver to assist and encourage children to read at all grade levels regardless of reading ability.

1. Create a daily reading routine. A reading routine provides the practice a child needs to reinforce and build reading and literacy skills.

2. Create a summer reading list. Choose a variety of children's books, including fairy tales, poems, fiction and non-fiction books.

3. Join or start a summer reading club. Check your local public library or bookstore.

4. Talk with your child about a book that you are reading. Let your child see how much you enjoy reading and ask them to share stories from some of their favorite books.

5. Children love to hear stories about their family. Tell your child what it was like when you or your parents were growing up, or talk about a funny thing that happened when you were their age. Have them share stories of their own about when they were "young."

Read 20 minutes a day!

CYBER READERS: Books in a Digital World

With the amount of electronic resources available, children are gaining access to subjects faster than ever before. With electronic resources comes a significant amount of "screen time" that children spend with technology including television, movies, computers, phones and gaming systems. It is important to manage "screen time" and include time for books. Reading a book helps develop attention spans and allows children to build their imaginations without the aid of animated graphics, special effects and sound that may hinder a child's ability to create these for themselves.

Summer Reading List – Fifth to Sixth Grade

Find the books listed here or on other summer reading lists at the library, bookstore or online. Look at both the front and back covers and read a few passages or paragraphs from inside the book. If it does not fit your interest or reading ability, find another book and repeat the process until you are happy with your choice of reading. Summer is as much a time to read for enjoyment, as it is to maintain reading skills while away from school. We recommend you read for a minimum of 20 minutes a day during the summer with the optimistic belief that once you find the perfect book you will not want to put it down- Happy Reading!

The key to a good summer reading list is having a wide variety of books that kids enjoy. In addition to this list, visit the library and let your child choose titles of their own. Ask the librarian for recommendations.

Al Capone Does My Shirts
By Gennifer Chodenko

Anne of Green Gables
By Lucy Montgomery

The BFG
By or any title by Roald Dahl

Because of Winn Dixie
By Kate DiCamillo

The Best School Year Ever
By Barbara Roberts

Black Beauty
By Anna Sewell

The Boggart
By Susan Cooper

The Book of Three
or any title By Lloyd Alexander

Brian's Return
By Gary Paulsen

Brian's Winter
By Gary Paulsen

Bridge to Teribithia or others
By Katherine Paterson

Bud, Not Buddy
By Christopher Paul Curtis

Catch That Pass
or any title by Matt Christopher

The Cay
By Theodore Taylor

White Chasing Redbird
By Sharon Creech

Chicken Soup for the Kid's Soul
By Jack Canfield

Crash
By Jerry Spinelli

Dear Mr. Henshaw
By Beverly Cleary

Dirt Bike Racer
By Matt Christopher

The Egypt Game
By Zilpha Keatley

Snyder Esperanza Rising
By Pam Munoz

Ryan Everything on a Waffle
By Polly Horvath

The Far Side of the Mountain
By Jean Craighead George

Fire Pony
By W. R. Philbrick

Flush
By Carl Hiaasen

The Gold Cadillac
By Mildred Taylor

Harriet the Spy
By Louise Fitzhugh

Harry Potter and the Sorcerer's Stone
By Rowling

Harry Potter and the Chamber of Secrets
By Rowling

Harry Potter and the Prisoner of Azkaban
By Rowling

Harry Potter and the Goblet of Fire
By Rowling

Hoot
By Carl Hiaasen

The Indian in the Cupboard
By Lynne Reid Banks

Inkheart
By Cornelia Funke

Inkspell
By Cornelia Funke

Into the Land of Unicorns
By Bruce Coville

Island of the Blue Dolphins
By Scott O'Dell

Julie of the Wolves
By Jean Craighead George

The Lion, the Witch, and the Wardrobe
By C. S. Lewis

A Little Princess
By Frances H odgkins Burnett

A Long Way from Chicago
By Richard Peck

The Lost Years of Merlin
By T. A. Barron

Lyddie
By Katherine Paterson

Skills Assessment Grade 5 - Reading

Directions: Circle the correct answer for each question.

1. Which sentence has correct capitalization?
A. Stone Mountain park is in Georgia.
B. Dr. Don Mathews is our principal.
C. My aunt is the Treasurer of the Club.
D. We are waiting for mrs. Kelly.

2. Which sentence has correct capitalization?
A. December is usually a cold month.
B. George called me last tuesday.
C. The Club meets every Saturday.
D. Jeff and I went to New York in may.

3. Which sentence has correct punctuation?
A. Jason wrote a story about dolphins!
B. Have you read the book Hatchet by Gary Paulsen.
C. Becky answered, "Yes, I am sure he will arrive on time."
D. My father asked, did you mow the lawn and clean out the garage.

4. Which sentence has correct punctuation?
A. The attorney Mr. Barker defended him.
B. Have the Clark's made their choice?
C. Will you assist your grandfather
D. Please dont send anymore text messages.

5. Which sentence has a misspelled word?
A. What is the populetion of New York?
B. The parachute opened rather quickly after he jumped from the plane.
C. The speaker used the auditorium.
D. Do you remember our trip to Kansas?

6. Which sentence has a misspelled word?
A. Mother's schedule is quite flexible.
B. Mrs. Duff had several good ideas to improve the cafeteria lunches.
C. My father has always said that Bert is such a mischevus boy.
D. Do you need to ask permission to go to Six Flags this weekend?

7. Which group of words is NOT a sentence?
A. Jason likes to play practical jokes.
B. The tall man wearing glasses is my father.
C. Have you been across the lake?
D. According to the contest rules.

8. Which group of words is NOT a sentence?
A. Our family is having fish and chips for dinner.
B. For capturing the bank robbers.
C. My friend spends money foolishly.
D. David set the plant carefully on the shelf.

9. What part of speech is the underlined word?
<u>Because</u> Jose did not finish the race, he was disqualified.
A. Noun   B. Preposition
C. Adjective   D. Conjunction

10. What part of speech is the underlined word?
<u>Whew!</u> I finished the paper just in time.
A. Preposition   B. Conjunction
C. Interjection D. Pronoun

11. What is the simple subject in the following sentence?
The north bound subway passes here every ten minutes.
A. north
B. subway
C. passes
D. minutes

12. What is the simple subject in the following sentence?
Chuck heard a strange noise in the basement.
A. Chuck
B. heard
C. noise
D. basement

Directions: Circle the correct answer for each question.

13. What is the complete predicate in the following sentence?

Aubrey likes to read science fiction novels.

A. Aubrey

B. likes to read

C. Aubrey likes to read

D. likes to read science fiction novels

14. What is the complete predicate in the following sentence?

Jennifer did not understand the directions.

A. Jennifer did not understand

B. Jennifer did not

C. did not understand the directions

D. understand the directions

15. Read each pair of sentences. Circle the answer that best combines the sentences.

We had a family picnic. The picnic was on Memorial Day.

A. On Memorial Day our family had a picnic.

B. We had a family picnic on Memorial Day.

C. On the Memorial Day was had a family picnic.

D. A family picnic was had on Memorial Day.

16. Read each pair of sentences. Circle the answer that best combines the sentences.

Tracy saw a weird animal. The animal was running down the sidewalk.

A. Tracy saw a weird animal running down the sidewalk.

B. The weird animal Tracy saw it running down the sidewalk.

C. Tracy saw a weird animal it was running down the sidewalk.

D. The weird animal Tracy saw it was running down the sidewalk.

Circle the answer for the word that has the same or almost the same meaning as the underlined word.

17. Found in this obscure book

A. mysterious

B. brilliant

C. little-known

D. objective

Circle the answer for the word that has the same or almost the same meaning as the underlined word.

18. A judicious choice of words

A. united

B. wise

C. gross

D. puzzling

Agreement of Subject and Verb: Select the correct form of the verb, either A or B which agrees in number with the subject.

19. One of my best friends (A. was, B. were) playing against me.

20. Some of these errors in your essay (A. is, B. are) preventable.

21. His objections to our evening program (A. seems, B. seem) trivial.

22. Working under these unfavorable conditions (A. is, B. are) exhausting.

Correct Use of Pronouns: Select the correct form of the pronoun, either A or B.

23. Oscar is older than (A. her, B. she).

24. Please wait for Tony and (A. I, B. me).

25. Ask Joseph and (A. he, B. him) to finish painting the bedroom.

26. Dad wants to know (A. who, B. whom) you voted for judge of the circuit court.

27. Is the captain (A. he, B. him) or Jeff.

28. Go ahead and (A. we, B. us) will follow.

29. Round to the nearest ten: 207,458

A. 200,000
B. 210,450
C. 207,460
D. 207,550

30. Compare: 45/9 _____ 36/4

   A. =
   B. <
   C. >

31. Round the sum of 45.84 + 36.02 to the nearest whole number.
   A. 81.0
   B. 82.1
   C. 81.2
   D. 82.0

32. Which best describes the number of faces on the figure below?

A.   faces = vertices   B.   edges = faces
C.   faces < vertices   D.   faces > edges

33. How many more sides are in an octagon and pentagon than one hexagon?

A. 8   B. 6
C. 7   D. 13

34. Which expression is true?
A. a + b = 6a
B. − a • − 6 = 12a
C. (a)6= 6a
D. a − 6 = -6a

35. Which equation is = to 45?
A. 3(3) + 15 = ☐
B.   9($\sqrt{25}$) = ☐
C. 45 + - 45 = ☐
D. - 2 (100) - 50 = ☐

36. Lisa spent $194.36 at the mall on Tuesday. Amanda spent $74.50 on Tuesday and half of that on Wednesday. Combined, what did the 2 girls spend?

A. 194.36 + 74.5 = ☐
B. 2(194.36) + 2(74.5) = ☐
C. 194.36 x 2(74.5) = ☐
D. 194.36 + 1.5(74.5) = ☐

37. Walt runs a 5k in 54.3 minutes If he improves his time by 20%, how many minutes is that?
A. 1.1086 min.
B. 1.086 min.
C. 10.86 min.
D. 1.860 min.

38. What is Walt's new time?
A. 44.34 min   B. 43.44 min
C. 34.44 min   D. 40.33

39. If nine 1 in. cubes were stacked in three congruent rows and columns, what would be the perimeter of that figure?
A. 16   B. 18
C. 12   D. 14

40. Compute: 764
                    x 14

A. 10,696   B. 10,596
C. 10,686 40   D. 10,736

41. Find the quotient: 874 ÷ 4 = _____
A. 219.0   B. 281.2
C. 218.5   D. 268.5

42. Choose the equivalent fraction for 16/12 in lowest terms.
A. 1 1/2   B. 1 1/4
C. 1 1/3   D. 2 1/2

43. Add. 1/2 + 3/4 = □
A. 1 1/2   B. 1 1/4
C. 1   D. 2 1/4

44. Subtract.   9/12 – 8/12 = □
A. 1 5/12   B. 1 1/12
C. 1 3/4   D. 1/12

45. Multiply. (1/3) * (2/9)
A. 2/27   B. 3/27
C. 3/9   D. 1/34

Find the Total Surface area of the rectangular prism that measures 8 ft. long, and its square base is 2 feet per edge.

A. SA = 4(4 x 8) x 2(4 x 4)
B. SA = 8(2 x 8) + 2 (4x 4)
C. SA = 4(8 x 4) + 2 (4 x 4)
D. SA = 8(4 x 4) x 2 (2 x 4)

47. Complete the function box.

x	x + 2
4	
	8
8	
10	
12	

48. Amy rolled two dice one time. What is the probability of her getting a 6 on one of the die?
A. 1/6   B. 2/6
C. 4/12   D. 1/3

49. If Mark makes 9.8 pretzels in one minute, how many will he make in 30 seconds?
A. 5.3 pretzels   B.   4.5 pretzels
C. 4.4 pretzels   D.   4.9 pretzels

50. Compute: 2(4)(-3) + 10 = _____
A. 34   B. -32
C. 12   D. -14

PARENT TIPS FOR WEEK 1

Skills of the Week

✔ Sentence or Sentence Fragment?

✔ Prepositions

✔ Reading Comprehension

✔ Conjunctions

✔ Geometric Shapes

✔ Periodic Table

✔ Interjections

✔ Geography

Weekly Value Honesty

Honesty means being fair, truthful, and trustworthy. Honesty means telling the truth no matter what. People who are honest do not lie, cheat, or steal.

Abraham Lincoln

Sometimes it is not easy to tell the truth, especially when you are scared and do not want to get in trouble or let others down. Try to remember that even when it is difficult telling the truth it is always the best way to handle any situation. People respect you more when you are honest.

GET FIT TIME!

Play 60 Every Day!
Run, jump, dance and have fun outside every day for 60 minutes!

Weekly Extension Activities at SummerFitLearning.com

Honesty In Action!
Color the star each day you show honesty through your own actions.

WEEK 1
HEALTHY MIND + HEALTHY BODY

Color the ☆ As You Complete Your Daily Task

		Day 1	Day 2	Day 3	Day 4	Day 5
🧠	**MIND**	☆	☆	☆	☆	☆
🏋️❤️	**BODY**	☆	☆	☆	☆	☆
📖	**DAILY READING**	☆	☆	☆	☆	☆
		20 minutes	20 minutes	20 minutes	20 minutes	20 minutes

You can do it!

"I am honest"

_____

Print Name

Sentence or Sentence Fragment?

A **sentence** is a group of words that expresses a complete thought. A sentence begins with a capital letter. A group of words that does not express a complete thought is called a **sentence fragment**.

Sentence or Sentence Fragment?   Identify each sentence by writing the letter **S** in the blank. If the group of words does not form a sentence, write **SF**.

_____ 1. Alex and Scott took their boat to the lake for the weekend.

_____ 2. When our neighbor arrived at our house before dark.

_____ 3. As the two women were cleaning the large house.

_____ 4. My two sisters were on their way from Chicago to New York.

_____ 5. Please wait quietly in the great room.

_____ 6. My entire family loves to eat pizza and cheese sticks.

_____ 7. After Joey and David played in the ball game.

_____ 8. Although Carlos was scared of heights, he climbed the ladder.

_____ 9. In the garage on the left side of your mother's car.

_____ 10. Please open the door for your grandfather.

Mixed Practice

1.	2.	3.	4.	5.
60	92	246	454	157
x 74	x 27	x 8	x 13	x 18

6.	7.	8.	9.	10.
8) 656	7) 1995	6) 1728	9) 1692	3) 6924

Aerobic
Go to www.summerfitlearning.com for more Activities!

DAILY EXERCISE
Jogging for Fitness 5
"Stretch Before You Play!"

Instruction
Jog 5 minutes in place or outside

Be Healthy!
Breakfast is the most important meal of the day!

DAY 1

WEEK 1

Prepositions

A **preposition** is a word that relates a noun or pronoun to other words in the sentence. The **object of a preposition** is the noun or pronoun that follows the preposition. A **prepositional phrase** is a group of words that begins with a preposition and ends with a noun or pronoun. Prepositional phrases often tell where, what kind, and how. Some commonly used prepositions are as follows:

about	above	across	after	around	before	below	behind	beside	except	for
from	in	near	on	of	off	out	over	through	to	under

Example: The chorus students met <u>behind the auditorium</u>.

Directions: Read each sentence. Underline each prepositional phrase.

1. After the concert everyone praised Cynthia for her performance.

2. Daniel had practiced every day before the concert tour.

3. Although Angela can sing like a bird, she is lazy about her voice practices.

4. The principal was behind the curtain during the performance.

5. When I talked with the principal, he said that he would let us know if we had won.

6. Angela and I are in the same math class, but her assignments are different from mine.

7. Carmen and Lydia sang behind me during the concert.

Read the passage. Then answer the questions.

The Gulf Coast Hot Air Balloon Festival welcomes more than 50 hot air balloonists from across the country. Enjoy the floating works of art as they grace the skies of South Baldwin County in Foley, Alabama. You can get up close and personal as the hot air balloons and their pilots light up the evening skies at the nightly balloon glows, held on Friday and Saturday night. Early morning flights (about 6:00 AM) are the best time to see the balloons. Balloons are also scheduled to fly at dusk (about 7:00 PM), weather permitting. Winds must be less than 10 knots for balloons to fly at dusk.

Guests enjoy free, fun entertainment featuring something for every member of your family. Spread out your blanket, grab an ice cold drink and enjoy a variety of live music daily, from country to rock and roll. Catch one of the many shows by the Disc Connected K-9 Frisbee Dog Show. Toss after toss you will be amazed as man's best friend defies gravity catching their prized flying saucers.

If you like, pet a baby alligator, dance like a butterfly to fun kid's tunes, paint your face like a tiger or try a little family friendly game of limbo. The free children's village offers hours of fun for any age. Or grab an ice cream cone or snack on popcorn as you stroll through the Arts & Crafts Village and Retail Marketplace featuring local crafters, artisans, and retailers. View daily demonstrations from crafters and chefs, find a one of kind piece of art, or grab a souvenir.

1. What is the main idea in this passage?

    A. Balloons are scheduled to fly at dusk (about 7:00 PM).

    B. You can get up close and personal as the hot air balloons light up the skies.

    C. The Gulf Coast Hot Air Balloon Festival welcomes more than 50 hot air balloonists.

    D. Guests enjoy free, fun entertainment featuring something for every family member.

2. Where is the Gulf Coast Hot Air Balloon Festival held? _____

3. There are so many different activities that you can enjoy. Which activities would you enjoy

the most? _____

_____

4. What is considered the best time of the day to view the balloons? _____

Strength Go to www.summerfitlearning.com for more Activities!

DAILY EXERCISE
Knee lifts
"Stretch Before You Play!"

Instruction
Repeat 5 times with each leg

Conjunctions

A **conjunction** is a part of speech used to connect words, phrases, or clauses. There are three kinds of conjunctions: **Coordinating conjunctions** connect words, clauses, or phrases of equal rank (for example: but, and, nor, for, so, yet). **Correlative conjunctions** are always used in pairs (for example: either . . . or, neither . . . nor, whether . . . or (not), both . . . and, not only . . . but also). **Subordinating conjunctions** connect dependent clauses with main clauses (if, unless, although, since, after, as, because, until, when, where, while, whenever).

Underline the conjunction in the following sentences. Then in the blank tell the type of conjunction.

_____ 1. You can count on Juan to eat either four or five slices of pizza.

_____ 2. Whenever it rains hard, our roof always leaks.

_____ 3. Although the math teacher was strict, she was quite fair.

_____ 4. Francisco has three brothers and two sisters in his family.

_____ 5. Amia's homework is both neat and accurate.

_____ 6. Because I did not finish my homework, I received an incomplete.

_____ 7. Roberta is going to the movie, but Isabella is going shopping.

_____ 8. Mrs. Barnard will pay you for the job whether she is here or at work.

_____ 9. Unless I study hard, I will fail this science test.

_____ 10. Either we will buy the television now, or we will wait for the next sale.

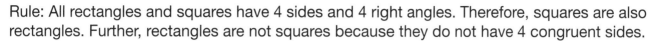
Rule: All rectangles and squares have 4 sides and 4 right angles. Therefore, squares are also rectangles. Further, rectangles are not squares because they do not have 4 congruent sides.

Task: Decompose the figures below to find the rectangle. Then use the referenced measurements to calculate the surface area using the area formula:

a = b(h) (where b = base and h = height).

1.   11 cm 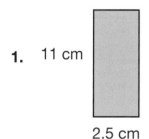   **A = _____**   **2.**   9 cm 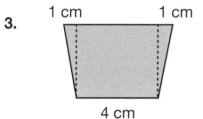   **A = _____**

   2.5 cm   5 cm

3.   1 cm   1 cm   **A = _____**   **4.**   .5 cm   **A = _____**
      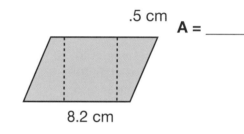

   4 cm   8.2 cm

Writing Activity

Using geometric terms and regular geometric figures, draw 2 shapes that resemble a sports field. Below each drawing, write in your own words a description of each image.

Figure 1   **Figure 2**

_____

_____

_____

_____

_____

DAILY EXERCISE
Jumping Jacks
"Stretch Before You Play!"

Instruction
20 Jumping Jacks

Be Healthy!
Ask your parents about what foods are good for you.

Periodic Table

Periodic Table of the Elements

Russian chemistry professor **Dmitri Mendeleev** and German Chemist **Julius Meyer** independently published their periodic tables in 1869 and 1870, respectively. They both constructed their tables in a similar manner: By listing the elements in a row or column in order of atomic weight and starting a new row or column when the characteristics of the elements began to repeat. All of the elements have been organized into a periodic chart that lets scientists study their similarities as well as differences. The letters inside each box represent the chemical symbol for the element. In the years following the publication of Mendeleev's periodic table, the gaps he identified were filled as chemists discovered additional naturally occurring elements. The number above the symbol is the atomic number of that element; whereas the number below the symbol is the atomic weight of that element.

Use the words in the box to complete the sentences.

elements	group	manner	number	period	properties	similar	symbol	weight

1. The periodic table organizes all of the _____.

2. The number above the symbol is the atomic _____ of that element.

3. The number below the symbol is the atomic _____ of that element.

4. The letters inside each box represent the chemical _____ for that element.

5. Each row going across the periodic table is called a _____, which shows how a sequence of properties repeats itself, similar to the days of the week.

6. Each row going down the periodic table is called an atomic _____ and all of these elements have similar _____.

7. Both Mendeleev and Meyer constructed their tables in a _____ manner.

Interjections are often used to show strong surprise or strong feelings. An interjection, followed by a comma or exclamation point, is independent of the other words in a sentence. If an interjection shows strong feeling, it is followed by an exclamation point.

Example: **_Hurry!_** The train is leaving the station.

Directions: In each sentence, underline the interjection.

1. Good grief! Did you eat all of the pie in one sitting?

2. Jessica seems to be unhappy. Oh, dear!

3. Good grief! That car needs too much work.

4. Hurrah! George passed the fifth grade.

5. Jason, where are you? Oops!

6. Goodness! I cannot stand all that noise.

7. Oh, my! How can you stop the bleeding?

8. Help! I dropped the priceless vase.

9. Ouch! That really hurt my ankle.

Prohibition Era - 1840-1920

The 18th Amendment of the US Constitution established prohibition in the United States. Legal uses of alcohol were only those for religious or medicinal purposes. Crime and undercover sales of alcohol increased tremendously. The political parties fought about ways to control yet consider the commerce benefits of legal alcohol sales.

Eventually the benefit of legal sales and distribution of alcohol gained popularity. Pauline Sabin, a Republican woman, convinced fellow Congress members to repeal the 18th Amendment with the 20th Amendment, which was the only instance of a repeal of an amendment in US history.

1. What is the goal of the 18th Amendment? _____

2. What problems did prohibition seem to create? _____

3. Why was the 18th Amendment repealed? _____

4. What positive impact did the Congress woman believe alcohol distribution and sale would

have? _____

DAILY EXERCISE
Chin-ups
"Stretch Before You Play!"

Instruction
Repeat 2 times

Be Healthy!
Talk about your day with your family.

Geography - On the Map

Where in the World is This Landmark?

Directions: By reading the clues, choose the correct landmark. Choose your answers from the box below.

1. I stand on the waterfront in the largest city in Australia, and I am one of the most recognizable images of the modern world. I have come to represent Australia.

   _____

2. The President's Mountain, honoring four US presidents, is located in the Black Hills of South Dakota. The monument was the brainchild of Doane Robinson. His goal was to create an attraction that would draw people from all over the country to his state.

   _____

3. One of the most famous attractions in the US, I am 279 miles (449 km) long and 1 mile (1.6 km) deep. People come from all over the world to hike in and around me.

   _____

4. I was built to house bells for a cathedral. I do not sit upright because the soil on which I was built was too soft. It took over 800 years to complete my structure in 1350.

   _____

5. Built about 4,500 years ago in Egypt, I stand 66 feet (20m) tall, and I am 240 feet (73 m) long. I am made out of limestone. Where I sit was once a quarry, and it is believed the workers used that quarry to shape the stone into the structure I am today.

   _____

6. I am often compared to a huge dragon winding up and down in the mountains, grassland and deserts. Over 20 Chinese states and dynasties built me to stretch 5,500 miles (8,854.8 km).

   _____

Mount Rushmore	Grand Canyon	Sydney Opera House
Leaning Tower of Pisa	Great Sphinx	Great Wall of China

WEEK 1

DAY 4

1 2 3 5

Honesty means doing what is right and fair to those persons involved and sometimes that can be unpopular among friends. Truthful attitudes and behaviors are key parts of being an honest person and result in one's actions.

Abraham Lincoln developed his reputation for honesty soon after leaving home at the age of 22. He worked as a storekeeper in 1831 for Denton Offutt. In 1832 he decided to run for the legislature but lost. Abe honestly represented himself to the citizens as a man of meager means and of no fame or popularity. He said his election would rest firmly on the people's belief in him.

In 1832 Lincoln joined William Berry as a partner in a general store venture. Berry became ill and soon died leaving Lincoln with a failed business and $1,000 of debt which was owed to many people. Lincoln eventually paid off the debt completely affirming statewide his honest ways. In 1834 he chose to run again for the legislature and won. At age 25 Abe was known for honesty and fairness in business and his promise to American politics.

Directions: Answer the following questions by filling in the blanks.

1. Abe Lincoln became a business partner at the age of _____.

2. Abe left home _____ years before he was elected to the state legislature.

3. Abe's business partner left him with a failed business and a large _____.

4. Abe Lincoln's first candidacy for the legislature was _____.

5. Being _____ to people was Lincoln's rule for business and politics.

Multimedia Resource:

Visit some websites of current day political leaders you like and read their blogs, comments or position statements. Consider how honest they are as compared to what you know about Abe Lincoln. Discuss what you find with someone whose opinions you trust. This person could be someone in your family, school, neighborhood, or even a local political activist. Often the best way to develop your attitudes and beliefs is not to merely copy someone else. Rather, figure out your own through research, personal experiences and discussions with people who have opposing views.

Choose 1 or more activities to do with your family or friends. Color today's star when you are finished. Good job!

☐ Read about someone who was known for their honesty (Confucious, Cochise, or Barbara Jordan are examples).

☐ Write a letter of thanks to a politician or leader in your community who has taken a stand on a controversial issue, or has kept their word.

☐ Thank someone you know for their honesty and truthfulness. Be truthful with your friends and family. Write an honesty motto or pledge for you and your family. Hang it where all can see.

Core Value Booklist
Read More About Honesty

The Skull of Truth
By Bruce Coville

Liar, Liar Pants on Fire
By Gordon Korman

Ruthie and the (Not So) Teeny Tiny Lie
By Laura Rankin

Honest Ashley
By Virginia L. Kroll

The Secret to Lying
By Todd Mitchell

Reading Extension Activities at SummerFitLearning.com

 Let's Talk About It

Encourage your child to be proud of who they are and help them understand that exaggeration is a form of dishonesty. Loyalty is important, but make sure they understand that keeping secrets is good as long as it is not about something that could hurt their friend or themselves. Talk about times when it is ok to tell on someone, and when it is not.

Stepping Stones

Stepping Stones Entertainment™ was founded by parents who wanted to provide meaningful family movies to help inspire common values. It is made up of people from many different backgrounds, nationalities and beliefs. For more than 20 years, Stepping Stones has provided families with movies about integrity, charity, forgiveness, and many other common values through hundreds of films for all ages. Learn more at **www.steppingstones.com**.

Play Time!
Choose a Game or Activity to Play for 60 minutes today!

YOU CHOOSE

_____
Write down which game or activity you played today!

 Be Healthy! Wash your hands before every meal.

1 2 3 4 **DAY 5** **WEEK 1**

PARENT TIPS FOR WEEK 2

Skills of the Week

✔ Verbs in Simple Tenses
✔ Place Value
✔ Word Problems
✔ Capitalization and Punctuation
✔ The Cell
✔ Population and Economics
✔ Texts abbreviation
✔ Planning

Weekly Value Compassion

Mother Teresa

Compassion is caring about the feelings and needs of others.

Sometimes we are so focused on our own feelings that we don't care how other people feel. If we consider other's feelings before our own the world can be a much kinder place. Take time to do something nice for another person and you will feel better about yourself.

GET FIT TIME!

Play 60 Every Day!
Run, jump, dance and have fun outside every day for 60 minutes!

Weekly Extension Activities at SummerFitLearning.com

Compassion In Action!
Color the star each day you show compassion through your own actions.

WEEK 2
HEALTHY MIND + HEALTHY BODY

Color the ⭐ As You Complete Your Daily Task

	Day 1	Day 2	Day 3	Day 4	Day 5
MIND	⭐	⭐	⭐	⭐	⭐
BODY	⭐	⭐	⭐	⭐	⭐
DAILY READING	⭐	⭐	⭐	⭐	⭐
	20 minutes	20 minutes	20 minutes	20 minutes	20 minutes

You can do it!

"I am compassionate"

_____
Print Name

In addition to showing action or linking subjects to the rest of the sentence, verbs indicate time. The time is, therefore, called **tense**. There are three tenses: present, past, and future.

Present tense verbs show action that is happening **now**.

Example: We **talk** on the cell phone for hours. (action verb)

Past tense verbs show action that happened **earlier**.

Example: Joyner **talked** on her cell phone for hours.

Future tense verbs show action that **will happen**.

Example: Paul **will talk** on his cell phone for hours.

Directions: Identify the tense of the underlined verbs in the following sentences. Write **PR** for present, **PS** for past, or **F** for future.

_____ 1. Two summers ago Amy <u>studied</u> Spanish in Mexico for six weeks.

_____ 2. Jerrell <u>will be studying</u> English in America this school year.

_____ 3. I <u>study</u> English every day in class.

_____ 4. Angelica <u>will help</u> you study Spanish if you help her study English.

_____ 5. The mountains <u>are</u> tall and beautiful in Wyoming.

_____ 6. Ernest Hemingway <u>wrote</u> "The Old Man and the Sea."

Sentence Structure

Directions: Read the sentence. What is the correct way to write this sentence?

7. Katy and Lydia skated to Alicia's house, and they play for an hour.

A. Katy and Lydia skated to Alicia's house, and they plays for an hour.

B. Katy and Lydia skated to Alicia's house, and they played for an hour.

C. Katy and Lydia skated to Alicia's house, and they playing for an hour.

D. Correct as written.

DAILY EXERCISE
Let's Jump
"Stretch Before You Play!"

Instruction
3 Sets of Jumps

DAY 1

Place Value Practice

Place value is the mathematical system that establishes quantity for numbers through a repeated pattern. Our number system is a base 10 number system. Therefore, each larger place value position is 10 times the previous position. Using this pattern of "times 10" larger, whole numbers can be easily identified.

Directions: Rewrite the following numbers increasing each one by 10 more units than the original, underlined digit.

1. 456,783 _____

2. 656,907 _____

3. 1,242,368 _____

4. 1,023 _____

5. 78,984 _____

6. 765,874,902 _____

7. 90,111 _____

8. 190 _____

Using what you know about place value patterns, find the digit 5 in each "original number" listed in the chart. Notice the "new number." Describe in your own words, how each number changed when only the 5 became 10 units greater.

9-13.

Original Number	New Number	What happened?
875	885	
7,152	7,252	
67,504	68,504	
435,212	445,212	
521	1,521	

Write the appropriate comparison symbol in the space provided to make each expression true. Use <, >, or =.

14. 905 _____ 509

15. 3,109 _____ 3,901

16. 76,345 _____ 76,543

17. 915 _____ 915

18. 89,741 _____ 89,714

19. 1,316 _____ 1,361

WEEK 2

Directions: Read each problem. Work each problem on a separate sheet of paper. Find the correct answer among the four possible answers. Write the letter next to that answer in the blank.

_____ 1. Ninety percent of the students in Mrs. Moore's fifth grade class had passing grades. If there were 30 students in the class, how many students failed?
A. 1
B. 2
C. 3
D. 4

_____ 2. Kenny studied from 6:00 to 7:15, from 8:00 to 9:30, and from 10:00 to 10:30. How long did Kenny study?
A. 3 hours 15 minutes
B. 3 hours
C. 2 hours 45 minutes
D. 3 hours 30 minutes

_____ 3. Mrs. Barker bought two heads of lettuce for 99¢, 3 pounds of bananas at $1.00 per pound, and a pound of apples at 99¢ a pound. How much did Mrs. Barker spend for the items?
A. $4.69 B. $4.97
C. $5.59 D. $5.97

_____ 4. Carl bought a used car for $4,800.00. He paid 6% sales tax, bought a tag for $55.00, and paid $450.00 for insurance. How much did he spend?
A. $5,593.00   B. $5,539.00
C. $5,439.00   D. $5,293.00

_____ 5. 5. The twenty-five students in Mr. Yun's class had a combined score of 2,200 on a math test. What was their average score?
A. 86 B. 88 C. 91 D. 92

_____ 6. Mason measured his cell phone cord and discovered it was 90.2 cm long. Leslie measured her school scarf, which was 113.75 cm in length. How much longer was Leslie's scarf than Mason's charging cell phone cord?
A. 23.75 B. 23.25
C. 23.55 D. 23.50

_____ 7. Tristan worked 5.5 hours for Mr. Cobb for $7.00 an hour. He then worked 6 hours for his grandfather for $5.25 an hour. How much money did Tristan make for working 11.5 hours?
A. $50 B. $60 C. $70 D. $80

_____ 8. The grocery store had milk on sale for $2.59 per gallon. How much would six gallons of milk cost?
A. $15.54
B. $15.45
C. $15.55
D. $15.64

_____ 9. Eli ran 100 meters in 14.5 seconds. If he could run at the same speed, how long would it take Eli to run 300 meters?
A. 45.5 seconds B. 43.5 seconds
C. 44 seconds   D. 43 seconds

_____ 10. Jason is 1.52 meters in height. Heath is 1.38 meters tall. How much taller is Jason than Heath?
A. 0.14 m   B. 0.13 m
C. 0.12 m D. 1.2 m

DAY 2

4

5

WEEK 2

Multimedia Task:
Write a humorous word problem about you and a friend, using any two operations (add, subtract, multiply or divide). Consider emailing/texting your friend to solve this problem. See if your friend emails/texts you with the answer as well as a word problem to solve.

DAILY EXERCISE
Bottle curls
"Stretch Before You Play!"

Instruction
**Repeat 5 times
with each arm**

Be Healthy!
Shop for food with your parents.

Capitalization and Punctuation

DAY
2

1

3

4

5

WEEK 2

Directions: Rewrite each sentence using the correct punctuation and capitalization.

1. Going to california was the best vacation Ive ever, had?

_____

2. "Before we leave this afternoon Be sure to feed the dog." Mom said,

_____

3. Mrs. Martin brought brownies to the party and She helped us clean up when it Was over.

_____

4. I think it would be fun to travel to London England one day? said Marcus.

_____

5. Conners portion of meat includes three pieces of chicken beef and fish.

_____

6. Where are your sandals?" Harriett asked her little sister."

_____

7. The soft sweet loving kitten purred as Jennifer picked her up.

_____

8. Yes thank you Steve. I will take care of making all of the arrangements?

_____

All living organisms are made of small life forms known as cells. Cells have specific purposes in function and structure and differ among plants and animals. This article will describe the similarities and differences in these two kinds of cells, as well as list other interesting work our cells perform. While both plant and animal cells contain a cell membrane, only the plant cell contains a cell wall. This cell wall surrounds the membrane. Both plant and animal cells have a nucleus. This is the "brain" of the cell. The nucleus contains the genetics of the cell and is the "boss" of the cell. The only part of the cell the nucleus cannot control is the membrane. Cell membranes control what comes in and out of the cell.

Through the lens of a compound microscope, it is possible to see these parts of a plant or animal cell. Many organisms are too small to be seen without magnification, and cells are certainly in this group. To better understand some basic parts of a cell, think of it as a piece of chocolate-coated candy with a peanut center. The outer candy coating is like the membrane, and the center peanut is like the nucleus. The chocolate between the outer coating and the peanut can be a metaphor for the cytoplasm. The cytoplasm contains important parts such as mitochondrion, the "energy center" of cells. In the case of a plant cell, imagine the wrapping paper of the candy as the cell wall.

Considering all of the parts of living things, their systems and functions for life-sustaining work, there is much to study and learn. Biology is the area of science that specifically involves the study of life. Cellular biology is a broad and important career field and many biologists work in labs every day doing exactly what you are beginning to learn on this page!

Animal Cell   **Plant Cell**

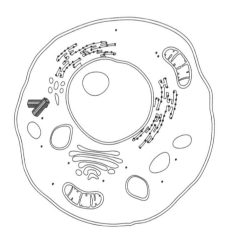
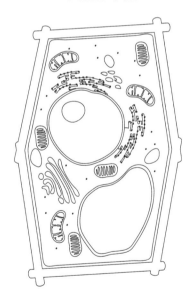

Directions:

After reading the passage, label each cell diagram with the proper term from the box below. Use lines or arrows to indicate the areas you are labeling.

cell membrane	cell wall	nucleus	cytoplasm	mitochondrion

DAILY EXERCISE
Let's Dance
"Stretch Before You Play!"

Instruction
Dance for 5 Minutes

Be Healthy!
Write down 3 healthy foods you like.

Population & Economics

Kelly was assigned a social studies project where she was to compare an American population to periods of time in history. She decided to compare United States military enrollment from the 1800's to 2006. Her study included finding data on enrolled members of the Army, Navy, Air Force and Marine Corps. In class she had learned about the American Civil War, the two World Wars, as well as the Korean and Vietnam conflicts. After reading her textbook, reviewing her class notes and researching many online government and military archives, Kelly had her project outlined and was ready to get started compiling her data. She chose to represent only three wars on her graph to show the growth and decline in military enrollment.

Kelly's report showed some stark differences. First, the number of enrolled military personnel changed drastically from the American Civil War to World War I. Then, from WWI to WWII there was a great decline in military participation. This decline was also an indication of the nation's diminishing economy. Women were unable to serve as much as they would be allowed in future wars.

Populations of Military Personnel

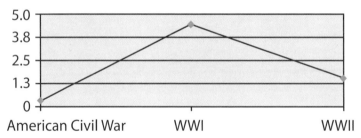

1. What is the biggest change the graph shows? _____

_____

2. Which World War had the highest population of enrolled personnel? _____

3. What prevented citizens from enrolling in the military? _____

_____

4. What economic difficulty was happening during WWI? _____

5. What branches of the military did Kelly research? _____

Using the currently popular "text-lingo," translate the messages below as if you are sending this message as a text to a friend of yours. Remember to make it as brief as possible. Text language is popular because it is brief and uses common and uncommon abbreviations. You may want to try this with a friend to see if your translations are similar.

> Hey Stan -
> It's me, Brian. I can't wait to go to the movie with you later tonight. My mom is on my case about something every day. I asked all week to go hang out with you guys, but she kept saying no because we had to take my dad to the airport. Of course, the next day we had to pick him up so that pretty much ruined my first two days. Oh, did you ever find that jacket I left at your house last weekend? If you did, please hold on to it for me. I think it's the only one that fits me right now. I definitely don't want to go shopping with mom, "the crazy shopper" this week! I will never get out of the mall if that happens! UGH! Ok dude - hit my cell phone when you are ready to go tonight. I will meet you there.
> Talk to you later!
> Brian

Translation:

_____

_____

_____

_____

_____

_____

_____

Strength Go to www.summerfitlearning.com for more Activities!

DAILY EXERCISE
Heel Raises
"Stretch Before You Play!"

Instruction
Repeat 8 times

Be Healthy!
Use sunscreen when you play outside!

Planning a Family Trip.

As a requirement to gain a badge for a club Jose was in, he needed to map out a trip for his family to take. The trip plan had to be prepared so that it would be at least fifty miles away from their hometown. It also had to include map directions, travel amenities along the way, places of interest, and a timetable. Jose decided on Bear National Park, which was over 60 miles from his hometown. He identified the roads they would travel, round-trip mileage, and rest stop locations.

Jose planned the family's travel in great detail. He used an online mapping tool to plan the route. He was also able to calculate the round trip mileage, identify preferred rest stops, and places of interest along the way. Jose's family chose to stay overnight at a nearby cabin community so they could enjoy the natural ambience of Bear National Park.

Jose's club leader considered his work extremely satisfactory and, therefore, earned him the badge for orienteering. Learning how to find places on a map in real life situations is important, and Jose discovered orienteering is very interesting and fun!

Use the chart below to plan and record details of a trip you would like to take, following the same rules Jose had to follow. Share this idea with your family. You may get to actually take this trip!

Our Trip Plan	
1. Destination:	
2. Miles: (round trip)	
3. Travel Time:	
4. Rest stop locations:	
5. Places of Interest:	
6. Accommodations:	

Compassion is a feeling of deep sympathy and sorrow for another who is stricken by misfortune, accompanied by a strong desire to alleviate the suffering.

During the years Mother Teresa compassionately served patients in small village hospitals, she learned many nursing skills. She was taught things, such as, the importance of proper nutrition, how to give patients injections, how to make "hospital corners" when making beds, and how to care for newborn babies. She was often needed to care for patients who had cholera or smallpox, and yet she remained personally healthy.

She saw great sadness as well as happier times. At first, Mother Teresa was afraid to hold newborn babies because she was worried she might hurt one. The nurses convinced her that even though they were small, they would love being held, and they would not "break." With practice and more skills, Mother Teresa became quite excellent at giving care to the sick. Her fellow hospital workers noticed how great she was at many tasks, especially her ability to remain calm during any crisis. Mother Teresa had compassion for others, and showed her work with the very sick people. Mother Teresa won many honors and awards for her work, including the Nobel Peace Prize.

Directions: After reading the passage above, answer the following questions.

1. What skills other than nutrition did Mother Teresa learn?

2. What conditions did some of her patients suffer?

3. How did Mother Teresa show compassion for the sick?

4. What was she worried about when caring for newborn babies?

5. Based on what this passage describes, what strength of Mother Teresa's impressed her colleagues?

Choose 1 or more activities to do with your family or friends. Color today's star when you are finished. Good job!

☐ Have a food drive to collect food for the food bank. Set up a time to volunteer at a local soup kitchen. Write about your experience and how it made you feel to help others.

☐ Make cards or crafts for people in the hospital or those in need. Plan a time to visit and spend time with them.

☐ Brainstorm with your friends or family. Write down as many words to describe compassion as you can think of, such as, sympathetic, empathetic, considerate, caring, gentle, tenderhearted, etc. Make a banner or poster and hang it up to remind everyone to be compassionate.

☐ Model compassion every day.

Core Value Booklist
Read More About Compassion

The Curse of Compassion
By Stephen Alexander Hammett

The Miracle Worker
By William Gibson

Because of Winn Dixie
By Kate DiCammilo

The View From Saturday
By E. L. Konigsburg

Shilo
By Phyllis Reynolds Naylor

Reading Extension
Activities at
SummerFitLearning.com

Let's Talk About It

We must encourage our children to go beyond feeling sad for someone. We must teach them to act on their feelings of sadness and act with compassion to do something to help others. Model compassion everyday: volunteer, give to charity, and practice random acts of kindness.

Play Time!

Choose a Game or Activity to Play for 60 minutes today!

YOU CHOOSE

Write down which game or activity you played today!

Be Healthy!
Plant a vegetable garden.

PARENT TIPS FOR WEEK 3

Skills of the Week

- ✔ Opinion
- ✔ Expressions and Symbols
- ✔ Perfect tenses
- ✔ Matter
- ✔ Government
- ✔ Inference
- ✔ Volume
- ✔ Synonyms and Antonyms

Weekly Value Trustworthiness

Harriet Tubman

Trustworthiness is being worthy of trust. It means people can count on you.

You are honest and you keep your word. Sometimes it is easy to forget what we tell people because we try to do too much or we are constantly moving around. Try to slow down and follow through on what you say before moving onto something else.

GET FIT TIME!

Play 60 Every Day!
Run, jump, dance and have fun outside every day for 60 minutes!

Weekly Extension Activities at SummerFitLearning.com

Trust In Action!
Color the star each day you show trustworthiness through your own actions.

WEEK 3

Color the ⭐ As You Complete Your Daily Task

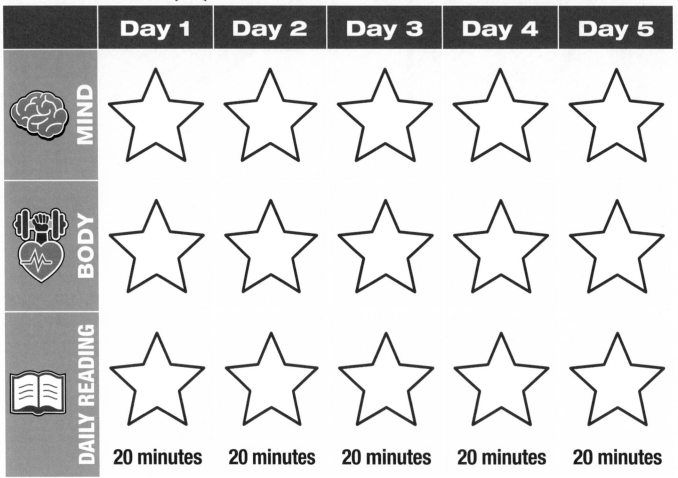

	Day 1	Day 2	Day 3	Day 4	Day 5
MIND	⭐	⭐	⭐	⭐	⭐
BODY	⭐	⭐	⭐	⭐	⭐
DAILY READING	⭐ 20 minutes	⭐ 20 minutes	⭐ 20 minutes	⭐ 20 minutes	⭐ 20 minutes

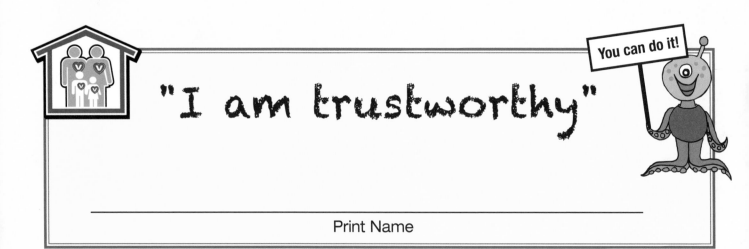

You can do it!

"I am trustworthy"

_____
Print Name

School Food

Our school food is lousy. There is simply no other way to describe it. Many students regularly bring their lunches because they refuse to eat the unsavory meals from the cafeteria. There are many complaints from students, and I agree with many of them. Just like any problem, there are usually two sides to the matter. I chose to speak to both sides in this dilemma: the students and the cafeteria manager. I found three main issues causing the conflict. These points of contention are the following: poor food quality and taste, food costs and food preparation time.

I found that food quality and costs and preparation times are closely related. The tastier and fresher the food, the more it costs and longer it takes to prepare. Our cafeteria has some very old equipment. Using these older ovens, stoves and refrigeration equipment creates a large electricity bill, and they often need repair. That costs the manager quite a bit of money from his budget. The cafeteria is expected to operate on the funds the lunches earn. I was surprised to find this out because I think many of us students thought the school system helped cover these costs. The cafeteria workers work an entire eight-hour day and paying employees is expensive, too.

To cut the budget so that our school cafeteria can operate, the manager had to order foods that are cheaper in costs. When we suggested new ways to earn money and offer new and better food choices, the manager was very excited about our ideas. Our suggestions would help his budget and make students happier at the same time. Using refrigerated vending machines to sell cold salads, sandwiches and fruit was one idea. This way the cafeteria workers could spend more time planning and preparing delicious and healthy recipes for hot entrees that students would enjoy. The beverages could also be sold from a beverage counter, or machine to eliminate extra work for the staff while making a profit as well.

This experience taught me that just because a problem exists, it does not mean it cannot be solved. I think by everyone sharing his/her ideas, we will be able to work with this information and find a way to make our cafeteria meals better for the students and our workers. Having healthy lunches that are good to eat is a wonderful way to help improve our school.

1 . What is the purpose of this writer's passage?

_____

2. Why was this writer motivated to write about school food?

_____

3. How did the writer develop the opinion that the food was lousy?

_____

4. Who else's opinions does the writer consider in this passage?

_____

Aerobic

Go to www.summerfitlearning.com for more Activities!

DAILY EXERCISE
Pass and Go
"Stretch Before You Play!"

Instruction
Get a Friend to Play this Game With You!

Be Healthy!
Eat breakfast with your family.

DAY 1

Expressions & Symbols

Note: An expression is a way of representing a value. Symbols such as brackets, parentheses, and signs of operations are used that serve as identification for the implied value.

Directions: Simplify the following expressions using what you know about numbers, symbols and signs of operation. Choose the value from the column on the right that best defines the expression.

_____ 1. (4 x 3)   A. 49

_____ 2. (1 x 5) – 2   B. 13

_____ 3. (7 – 2)   C. 3

_____ 4. 2(40 - 30)   D. 576

_____ 5. 7^2 E. 7

_____ 6. (56/8) + (6 – 2)   F. 29

_____ 7. [(9 x 3) –2] + 4   G. 20

_____ 8. (10 – 5) + 8   H. 5

_____ 9. 21/3   I. 11

_____ 10. $6^2(4^2)$ J. 12

Simplify the following expressions where x = 2 and y = 5.

11. 9x +2 = _____   12. x (4^2 - 2) = _____

13. 8 + y = _____   14. (3 –1) + y = _____

15. (y – 2) (4) = _____   16. (x + y) –1 = _____

17. (9)(9) – y = _____   18. (y)(2+3) = _____

19. [4(2x)] / 2 = _____   20. (x + 1) + 5 = _____

Multimedia Correlation: Visit a math teacher's website to see what category he/she lists this kind of activity. (Hint: It is the beginning of Algebra, working with variables and solving multi-step computations.)

WEEK 3

44 © Summer Fit

Present Perfect Tense places an action or condition in a time period leading up to the present. The tense is formed by using <u>has/have</u> with the **past participle**.
Example: The scientists <u>have traveled</u> to more than fifty countries to collect data.

Past Perfect Tense places a past action or condition before another past action or condition. This tense is formed by using **had** with the **past participle**.
Example: Before I went swimming, I **had finished** cleaning my bedroom.

Future Perfect Tense places a future action or condition before another future action or condition. This tense is formed by using **will have** with the **past participle**.
Example: Dr. Mason **will have conducted** an ongoing research before announcing his results.

Identify the perfect tense(s) of the underlined predicates (verbs) by writing the tense in the blank.

1. Jonathan said that he <u>had</u> already <u>seen</u> this movie before. _____

2. By one o'clock my sister <u>will have finished</u> the crossword puzzle. _____

3. I <u>have enjoyed</u> working in the garden each morning. _____

4. By noon, Martha <u>will have baked</u> three pecan pies today. _____

_____

Decimal Fractions on a Number Line

The adjacent boxes below are a part of a table. Think of the horizontal row of boxes as a number line. Use the spaces to record the correct decimal fractions from those given in the white space below the diagram. If there is not a correct, consecutive number, the tic mark on the number line should be left blank.

0   .25   ½   1   1.25   3.0

Decimal fractions to place on the number line:

3.5	¾	1 ½	2.75	1.75
3.25	3 ¾	2	2 ¼	2 ½

Strength
Go to www.summerfitlearning.com for more Activities!

DAILY EXERCISE
Squats
"Stretch Before You Play!"

Instruction
Repeat 6 Times

Be Healthy!
Drink small amounts of water while playing.

What Exactly Changed

Most everyone knows that all "stuff" is made up of what scientists call matter. That means the "stuff," or matter, can be anything. It commonly exists in three forms: solids, liquids and gases. Matter is made of small building blocks called molecules. Molecules combine to create a kind of matter that is specific. Matter can experience change. These changes may be physical or chemical. The difference in a physical change and a chemical change is in the kind of matter that results.

With a physical change, molecules can be arranged. They may be rearranged, thus forming a different appearance or an entirely different state of matter. When a solid ice cube melts, it is still water. The difference is that it is in a different form or state. The kind of matter is the same and the molecules are the same. Some other ways physical changes occur are as follows: cutting wood, crushing a drink can or even tearing a piece of paper. These are all still the same things although they have been changed physically. Physical changes may be reversed. This is referred to as a reversible change. For example, if an ice cube melts, re-freezing it makes it go back to the previous, solid state, an ice cube. A metal item can also be bent back to be much like it was originally. Scientists study physical changes because it helps understand all kinds of change.

A chemical change means a kind of matter has changed so entirely that a new kind of matter is formed. This change is irreversible. Some examples of chemical changes are making a cake, burning wood, or the process of photosynthesis. Chemical changes involve a kind of "reaction" that does cause the molecules to change so completely when combined with other things; it is nothing like the original. For example, when the ingredients for a cake are all combined to make the batter, the eggs, oil, sugar, flour and other ingredients combine to create cake batter. After baking in the oven, the cake batter is then changed to a brand new kind of matter, a delicious cake! Cooking is a broad area where many chemical changes may be observed.

Directions:

Complete the table below. Indicate the type of change that would result by writing "physical" or "chemical" in the corresponding boxes.

Example:	Type of change:	Result:
1. tearing up a cardboard box		
2. burning wood		
3. making pancakes		
4. ice cream melts		
5. broken flower pot		
6. cooking an egg		
7. rust on a nail		

DAY 2

1 3 4 5

WEEK 3

© Summer Fit

Historical Places in Washington D.C.

The Constitution of the United States has formed American politics, lifestyle, and education for over 200 years. It is the most revered object for almost all Americans and admired by people worldwide. William Gladstone said many years ago that this work was the most wonderful creation by people at a given time by the brain and purpose of mankind. To this day, we honor our constitution and all that it embodies.

The Preamble of the Constitution is a brief writing, but again it reminds us of the type of governmental freedom our country was founded upon. It only consists of fifty-two words. This document as well as The Declaration of Independence, The Bill of Rights, hand-written letters from past U.S. Presidents, and many others are housed in Washington D.C. at the National Archives and Records Administration Building. This museum houses important government papers both past and present. There is no admission charge to visit this museum, and it is often a top priority of places to visit when traveling to our nation's capital.

Many other government buildings are top tourist spots as well and are equally accessible to U.S. tourists. The geographic design on which the city of Washington, D.C. is built is called a grid. A grid design for a city means that there are square blocks creating the pattern for the city's roads, and buildings are carefully planned to be constructed in particular areas. Using such a grid system, it is easy to memorize this sort of design because of its regular shape and relationship to cardinal directions of north, south, east and west.

In geometry the upper right quadrant of the whole coordinate plane is used to begin teaching such skills as coordinate locating, or plotting or "ordered pairs." On such a graph, the horizontal line represents the "x" axis and the vertical line, perpendicular to the x axis, is the "y" axis. Used in coordination, map locations are easily found.

DAY
3

5

WEEK 3

Directions: Decide if the following statements are true or false. Write a T or F on the line for each.

_____ 1. The Preamble is a brief historical document that contains only about 50 words.

_____ 2. The National Archives and Records Administrative building is basically a museum.

_____ 3. Many tourists find it confusing to travel around the city of Washington, D.C.

_____ 4. The Constitution of the United States is located in the White House.

_____ 5. Past U.S. Presidents whose letters are on display are interesting to many visitors.

Aerobic

DAILY EXERCISE
Step It Up
"Stretch Before You Play!"

Instruction
Start Slow &
Increase Your Speed

Be Healthy!
Eat different types to get all the nutrients you need!

Making Inferences

Inference is using information that is stated in a passage to draw a conclusion that is not stated. For example: After Edward broke the trophy, his father turned and walked away without saying a word. You might conclude or infer that Edward's father was upset–and that would be an inference. To infer means to arrive at a conclusion by reasoning from the evidence.

Synonyms for "infer" are conclude, deduce, or judge. If you are being told to infer something from a passage, then you are being asked what conclusions can be drawn from the context of the story or passage.

Directions: Read the following passages. Then select the best answer.

1. One of the missions of the Peace Corps is to help people of interested countries meet their need for trained men and women. People who work for the Peace Corps do so because they want to; however, to keep the agency dynamic with fresh ideas, no staff member can work for the agency for more than five years.

This passage best supports the statement that the Peace Corps employees

A. are hired for a limited term of employment.

B. must train for about five years.

C. are highly intelligent people.

D. have both academic and work experience.

2. Due to the incredible force and unpredictability, floods can cause tremendous damage. They can ruin houses, buildings, and roads. Floods can take down trees and cause mud slides. It often leaves mud, sand, and debris behind. After a flood, it can take months to clean up.

Based on what you have read, you can infer or conclude that

A. after flood waters dry up, then the problem is over.

B. floods only occur along the coastlines.

C. floods are not that dangerous.

D. cleaning up after a flood can be expensive and can take time.

© Summer Fit

Volume is the space inside a three dimensional figure. This is measured in cube units. The example below is a rectangular prism, or "box" divided into squares, or "cubes" to represent what is being measured in the calculations.

length = 5cm cubes

width = 2cm cubes

height = 2cm cubes

Volume can be found by stacking unit cubes. When it is not possible to find the volume of a container, a formula is used. The formula for finding volume of a rectangular prism is shown below the diagram on the right.

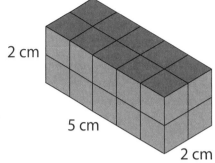

2 cm

5 cm

2 cm

$$V = l \times w \times h$$

Directions:

Find the volume for each figure below. Use the formula when necessary.

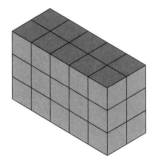

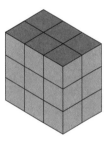

1. V = _____ cm³

2. V = _____ cm³

3. V = _____ cm³

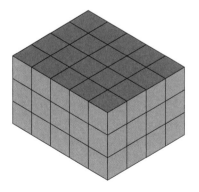

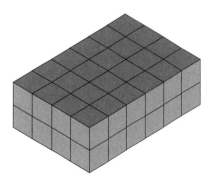

4. V = _____ cm³

5. V = _____ cm³

DAY
4

WEEK 3

Strength
Go to www.summerfitlearning.com for more Activities!

DAILY EXERCISE	Instruction
Lunges	**Repeat 5 times**
"Stretch Before You Play!"	**with each leg**

Be Healthy!
Drinking milk builds strong bones and teeth!

1
2
3
DAY
4
5

WEEK 3

Synonyms and Antonyms

A **synonym** is a word that has almost the same meaning as another word.
Examples: big, large, huge, gigantic

An **antonym** is a word that means the opposite of another word.
Examples: big—little; tall—short; straight—crooked

Directions: Choose the best synonym for the following words.

1. determine _____ behold, think, contemplate, ascertain, ponder

2. establish _____ destroy, construct, regret, create, build

3. urge _____ force, encourage, enter, attend, entice

4. decide _____ think, stay, choose, waver, equivocate

5. teach _____ educate, learn, endure, uphold, appeal

Directions: Choose the best antonym for the following words.

6. overthrow _____ elect, oust, surrender, undermine

7. confuse _____ puzzle, restore, misinform, explain

8. detect_____ expose, disguise, recognize, overlook

9. sluggish _____ aware, lazy, lively, sensitive

10. pardon_____ forgive, convict, relieve

Trustworthiness is a trait of deserving trust and confidence. A form of trustworthiness is being answerable to someone for something or being responsible for one's conduct or reliability.

Risking capture and sometimes death at every turn, Harriet Tubman led more slaves to freedom than anyone else in American history. Born into slavery (meaning she had no property, no rights, and had to do whatever her master told her) on a Maryland plantation in 1820, she first attempted to escape at the age of seven but was caught, beaten, and was put to work as a field laborer.

Twenty years later, Harriet finally made her way to the free North. Tubman began her career as a conductor on the "Underground Railroad," a highly secretive network of northerners who helped runaway slaves. Between 1850 and 1860, due to her trustworthiness, she returned to the South to guide more than 300 blacks, including her parents, to freedom.

At the outbreak of the Civil War, she helped the Union army in South Carolina. As a nurse, she cared for thousands of newly freed slaves; as a spy, she made deep inroads into enemy territory; as a commando, she led a series of devastating raids on Confederate positions. Popularly called "the Moses of her people," Harriet Tubman, truly known for her trustworthiness, was motivated by her sense of justice and duty rather than a desire for personal gain or glory.

Directions: Fill in the blanks using word(s) from the Harriet Tubman story.

1. Harriet Tubman led more slaves to _____ than anyone else in American history.

2. Tubman began her career as a conductor on the _____ _____.

3. Due to her trustworthiness, she guided more than _____ blacks, including her parents to freedom.

4. Harriet first attempted to escape slavery at the age of _____.

5. She has often been called "the _____ of her people."

6. At the outbreak of the Civil War, Tubman helped the Union army in _____ _____.

7. Tubman was motivated by her sense of _____ and _____ rather than desire.

8. During those years of the Civil War, she was classified as a _____, as a _____ and as a _____.

© Summer Fit **51**

☐ It takes a long time to develop trust, but it takes very little to lose it. Once a promise has been broken or a person shows he/she is not trustworthy, it is hard to rebuild that trust. Play the game JENGA, or use blocks or cards to make a tower as tall as you can. All it takes is one wrong move and the tower collapses, just like trust.

☐ Play a trust game with your family or friends. Make an obstacle course in the yard. Take turns blindfolding each other and leading each other through the course. Is it hard to trust someone?

☐ Sign up to volunteer somewhere and follow through on your commitment. Some examples are a food bank, a church, or homeless shelter. Part of being trustworthy is keeping your promises and honoring your commitments. Practice keeping your word and doing what you say you will.

Core Value Booklist
Read More About Trust

The Light at Tern Rock
By Julia Sauer

A Grain of Rice
By Helena Clare Pittman

The Apple and the Arrow
By Conrad Buff

Stepping on the Cracks
By Mary Downing Hahn

Reading Extension Activities at SummerFitLearning.com

Let's Talk About It

Children support their friends and in return depend on them for support. Talk with your children about the qualities you would like to see in their friends. Ask your child about the qualities of their friends and ask for examples of when they displayed them. What does your child think is the best quality in his/her friend(s)? Ask your child if he/she considers it to be a trustworthy quality.

Play Time!
Choose a Game or Activity to Play for 60 minutes today!

YOU CHOOSE

_____

Write down which game or activity you played today!

Be Healthy!
Ask your parents to teach you more about eating healthy!

WEEK 4

Skills of the Week

- ✔ Plate Tectonics
- ✔ Geometric Terms
- ✔ Misspelled Words
- ✔ U.S. Economics
- ✔ Multiplication and Division
- ✔ American History
- ✔ Advertising
- ✔ Idioms

Weekly Value
Self-Discipline

Stephanie Lopez Cox

Self-discipline, which means self-control, is working hard and getting yourself to do what is important.

It is easy to lose interest in what you are doing, especially if it does not come fast and easy. Focus your attention on what you are trying to accomplish and try to block out other things until you reach your goal.

GET FIT TIME!

Play 60 Every Day!
Run, jump, dance and have fun outside every day for 60 minutes!

Weekly Extension Activities at SummerFitLearning.com

Self-Discipline In Action!
Color the star each day you show self-discipline through your own actions.

WEEK 4

Color the ⭐ As You Complete Your Daily Task

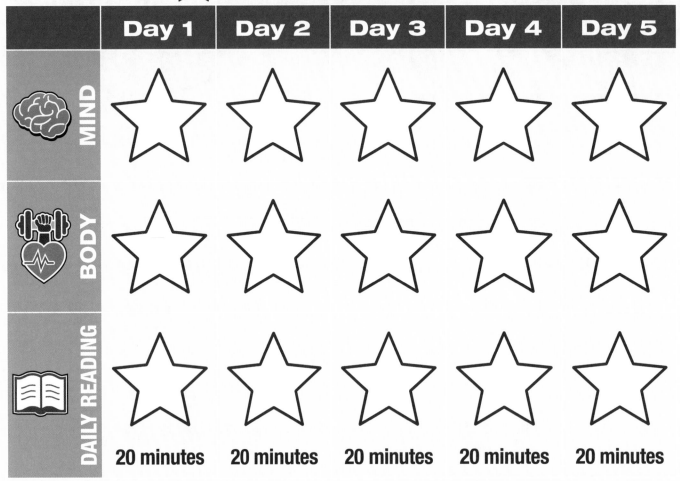

	Day 1	Day 2	Day 3	Day 4	Day 5
MIND	☆	☆	☆	☆	☆
BODY	☆	☆	☆	☆	☆
DAILY READING	☆ 20 minutes	☆ 20 minutes	☆ 20 minutes	☆ 20 minutes	☆ 20 minutes

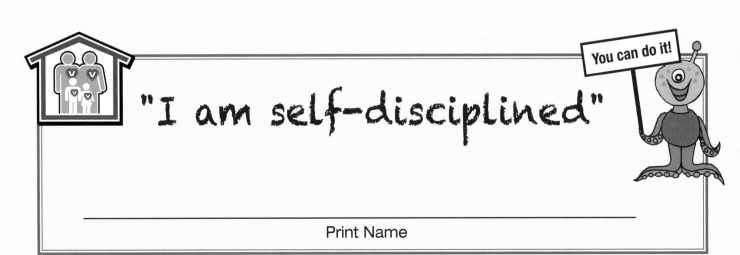

You can do it!

"I am self-disciplined"

Print Name

Plate Tectonics

Earth's interior is very hot. Heat flows and movement of inner earth material can cause abrupt changes to the earth's surface such as volcanoes and earthquakes. These dramatic changes to our earth result in new landforms, such as mountains and ocean basins. Slower occurrences of change are found in weathering. When wind and water move over the land over time, mountain ranges become leveled.

The continents and the ocean basins make up the solid crust of the earth. The layer beneath is made of a denser, hot and less deformable landform known as plates. Plates protect the crust from inner-earth material and slightly "float" over the earth. This movement of one or more plates can create a push or pull against other plates when in close contact. Plates forcing against each other may ultimately cause a shift that makes an ocean floor plate slide under a continental plate. This occurrence makes the plate sink deep into the earth. When these surface layers fold, mountain ranges may be formed.

Earthquakes often occur along the boundaries between colliding plates, and molten rock from below creates pressure that is released by volcanic eruptions. Volcanic eruptions help build up mountains. Under the ocean basins, molten rock amasses between separating plates. This creates a new ocean floor. Volcanic activity along the ocean floor may form undersea mountains, which can thrust above the ocean's surface to become islands.

Directions: The following chart categorizes key terms from the passage. Complete the chart by filling in data that refers to the particular headings. Refer to the reading passage as needed to accurately record the information. Use words, phrases, or sentences to relate your understanding.

	Crust	Plates	Landform
1.	Ex. mountains	"float"	mountains
2.			
3.			
4.			
5.			
6.			
7.			

DAILY EXERCISE
Kangaroo Bounce
"Stretch Before You Play!"

Instruction
Jump 10 Times

Be Healthy!
A calorie is a unit of energy.

DAY 1

WEEK 4

Geometric Terms

Directions: Match the geometric term with its definition.

____ 1. parallel lines

____ 2. diameter

____ 3. vertex

____ 4. radius

____ 5. circumference

____ 6. obtuse angle

____ 7. parallelogram

____ 8. perpendicular line segments

____ 9. acute angle

____ 10. right angle

____ 11. line segment

____ 12. point

____ 13. rhombus

____ 14. chord

____ 15. equilateral triangle

A. An angle greater than 90 degrees but less than 180 degrees.

B. An angle less than 90 degrees but greater than 0 degrees.

C. A 90 degree angle.

D. A line segment joining two points on a circle's circumference and passes through the circle's center.

E. Two line segments which cross to form 90 degree angles.

F. The line segment between two points on a given curve.

G. Line segments that do not intersect.

H. One part of a line.

I. A quadrilateral having both pairs of opposite sides parallel to each other.

J. An equilateral parallelogram having oblique angles.

K. A straight line extending from the center of a circle or sphere to the circumference.

L. The intersection point of two sides of a plane figure.

M. A position in space.

N. A triangle with all sides equal and all angles equal.

O. The distance around a circle (the perimeter).

Directions: Carefully look at each group of words and find the misspelled word. Circle the word that is misspelled. Then write the word correctly on the line.

1. A. childish   B. generus   C. language   D. similar   1. _____

2. A. preserved   B. fountain   C. agreeable   D. treazures   2 _____

3. A. balanket   B. wonderful   C. seventy   D. festival   3. _____

4. A. invitation   B. insterment   C. exercise   D. selected   4. _____

5. A. consisting   B. loseing   C. portion   D. patterns   5. _____

6. A. excelent   B. adjective   C. priceless   D. although   6. _____

7. A. minister   B. princess   C. threten   D. fountain   7. _____

8. A. chocolate   B. infermation C. rehearse   D. employment   8. _____

9. A. regardless   B. astonish   C. requires   D. earlyest   9. _____

10. A. generation   B. farewell   C. happyness   D. argument   10. _____

Directions: Circle the letter for the word that is spelled correctly and best completes the sentence. Then write the correct word in the blank provided.

11. The governor gave a _____ speech.
    A. pursuasive   B. perswasive   C. persuasive   D. perswasive

12. My parents celebrated their fifteenth _____.
    A. aniversary   B. anniversary   C. anniversy   D. anniversery

13. It is your _____ to tell the truth about the fire.
    A. obligation   B. oblegation   C. oblagation   D. oblagition

14. Our class _____ our plan for the homecoming parade.
    A. subbmitted   B. submited   C. submitted   D. subbmited

15. Of all my cousins, Amanda is the most _____ person.
    A. considurate   B. conciderate   C. considerete   D. considerate

Strength
Go to www.summerfitlearning.com for more Activities!

DAILY EXERCISE
Push-ups (traditional or modified)
"Stretch Before You Play!"

Instruction
Repeat 10 times

Be Healthy!
Remember to say "thank you" to your friends and family.

U.S. Economics

CRASH!

In 1929 the United States was enjoying an enthusiastic time. The war had just ended, the airplane and radio had been invented and many people felt their dreams might really be possible. Productivity flourished and people began to have more interest in investing money. They chose to pull their money out of banks and put it in the stock market. Once considered a risky investment, now the stock market had the appearance of a "fail proof" investment for the future. More and more people invested in the stock market, and it began to rise. The strong market, known as a "bull market," meant prices were rising and this made investors want to try this money-making opportunity. The booming market was alive and well in 1928.

This strong stock market changed the way people looked at investing money. Instead of the market being a long-term investor's tool, it became a hopeful ideal for everyday people hoping to get rich. With an increasing number of "ordinary" people wanting to make money buying stocks, there were some who did not have enough money to do this. That was the time when stock brokers began selling "on margins." This required the buyer to pay some of his own money toward the stock price, usually 10-20%. The remaining price of the stock (80-90%) would be paid by the broker. This kind of stock purchase could be very risky because of the chance that the stock's price could fall. If this happened and the value dropped below the amount of the loan, the broker could issue a demand to repay the loan called a "margin call." This would require the buyer to find the cash to pay back his loan immediately!

In early 1929 the stock market was still strong and more investors were participating. However, in March a mini-crash happened. The Dow Jones Industrial Average dropped, but it came back during the summer and things were fine through the month of August. On September 3, 1929 the market hit an all time high of closing at 381.17. Two days later, it began dropping. Sadly, on Thursday, October 24, 1929 the stock market crashed. Everyone had rushed to sell their stocks and the stock prices were dropping fast. That day is forever known as "Black Thursday," the day the stock market crashed and started the Depression Era for the U.S.

Directions: Answer the following questions with information from the passage.

1. What was the benefit of buying stocks "on a margin?" _____

2. When did the mini-crash happen? _____

3. From whom did people buy stocks? _____

4. What different kind of investors did the 1929 market attract?_____

5. What causes a "margin call" from a broker? _____

6. What is the name of the U.S. stock exchange?_____

7. What day is October 24, 1929 called?_____

Find the products.

1.	56 x 53	**2.**	76 x 38	**3.**	91 x 64	**4.**	55 x 47
5.	90 x 65	**6.**	174 x 32	**7.**	431 x 40	**8.**	1,255 x 16
9.	616 x 38	**10.**	2,291 x 17	**11.**	205 x 46	**12.**	902 x 37

Find the quotients (to the nearest hundredth).

13. 22 ⟌ 486

14. 16 ⟌ 4,868

15. 14 ⟌ 2,814

16. 30 ⟌ 7,936

17. 42 ⟌ 9,735

18. 26 ⟌ 8,641

DAILY EXERCISE
Hoops
"Stretch Before You Play!"

Instruction
Play to 11 by 1's

Be Healthy!
Instead of playing a video game play a board or card game.

American History

Directions: The following phrases refer to an invention in American history. Using the information, fill in the number line with the accurate date and corresponding information.

- The Cotton Gin: 1794 by Eli Whitney
- The Winchester Repeating rifle: 1854
- First submarine: 1776
- First reaping machine: 23 years before the rifle
- Telegraph: 1844
- Telephone: 32 yrs. after the telegraph
- Lockstitch sewing machine: 1883

- First electric fan: 1882
- Dishwasher: 7 years after the electric fan
- The zipper: 1893
- First digital computer: 1939
- Airplane: 36 years before the computer
- The first rocket: 1926
- Television: one year later than the rocket

		telegraph invented							airplane invented			
1794			1844					1893				

Use the data you populated in the timeline to answer the following questions.

1. What happened later, the invention of the sewing machine or the electric fan? _____
_____

2. What event on this time line follows the invention of the telegraph? _____
_____

3. Which events happened earliest and latest according to this time line? _____
_____

4. What invention precedes the dishwasher by 6 years? _____
_____

5. Which of these inventions occurred in the 19th century? _____
_____

6. What two events on this time line have the least amount of time between them?
_____

Directions: In the space below, design a magazine ad to lure Europeans to visit one of the 13 original colonies. Simply research one of the 13 original colonies. Using the facts that you have discovered, design a catchy magazine ad enticing Europeans and other settlers to visit one of the colonies. Include the following information: location, natural resources, food preparations, crops, schools, churches, transportation (i.e., buggies), and other interesting features.

DAILY EXERCISE
Crunches
"Stretch Before You Play!"

Instruction
Repeat 5 times

Be Healthy!
A healthy diet helps fight off sickness.

 Idioms

An **idiom** is a construction of words or a phrase that means something different than what the words are literally saying. Idioms have been passed down through tradition, culture, and history. Knowing and using idioms can improve your comprehension.

Example: to pay through the nose means someone has paid more money for something than what it is worth

Directions: What is meant by the following common idioms?

1. To make ends meet: _____

2. When it rains, it pours: _____

3. To pull your weight: _____

4. Great minds think alike: _____

5. Pull the wool over someone's eyes: _____

6. A piece of cake: _____

7. To take someone under your wing: _____

8. Bite off more than you can chew: _____

9. Let the cat out of the bag: _____

10. All bark and no bite: _____

11. Saved by the bell: _____

12. Haste makes waste: _____

13. To get out of hand: _____

14. When it rains, it pours: _____

15. To throw in the towel: _____

DAY 4

WEEK 4

1 2 3 5

Photo courtesy of Stephanie Lopez Cox

Self-discipline is having control of your actions and, therefore, focusing on your goals. Self-discipline includes having self-control, dedication, and commitment to the people and things that are important to you.

Growing up in Elk Grove, California, **Stephanie Lopez Cox** helped lead her high school soccer team to two league championships. She was named to the all-section team as a junior and senior, won the youth All-American award from NSCAA and was named a Parade Magazine All-American. Even though she is known for her superb soccer skills, she also lettered in basketball all three years of high school. Through her self-discipline and dedication, Stephanie played on the U.S. National Women's Soccer Team and lead her team to win the gold medal at the 2008 Beijing Summer Olympics.

Stephanie has assisted her parents in leading a group of teens to Egypt to paint an orphanage, traveled to the Bahamas to clear land for construction of a learning center, traveled to Mexico to serve meals to American missionaries, and was part of a team that created a Hurricane Katrina fundraiser in 2005. Stephanie recently became a spokesperson for Casey Family Services, the country's largest foster care organization. One can easily say that through her self-discipline Stephanie Lopez Cox is dedicated to bettering the world around her.

Directions: From the passage above, answer the following questions.

1. Even though Stephanie is known for her superb soccer skills, what else did she accomplish

   three years in high school? _____

2. Of the many accomplishments of Stephanie Lopez Cox, what was her greatest

   accomplishment? _____

3. List at least three other accomplishments in Stephanie Lopez Cox's life:

   _____

   _____

   _____

Choose 1 or more activities to do with your family or friends. Color today's star when you are finished. Good job!

☐ Give up TV for a day, a week, or longer. Instead, spend time outside, reading, or with friends and family.

Core Value Booklist
Read More About Self-Discipline

On the Field with ... Mia Hamm
By Matt Christopher

No Limits: The Will to Succeed
By Alan Abrahamson

A Chair for My Mother
By Vera B. Williams

The Karate Kid
By B. B. Hiller

The Book of Virtues (for Young People)
By William J. Bennett

Reading Extension Activities at SummerFitLearning.com

☐ Plant a small flower or vegetable garden. Be disciplined every day in watering and weeding your garden.

☐ Practice self-discipline with your money. Instead of spending the money you earn, save up for something special.

☐ Make a list of how you can show self-discipline in taking care of your body: your eating habits, exercise, and hygiene. Make a chart of ways you can be healthy. Practice self-discipline and stick to your goals.

Let's Talk About It

Self-discipline is a difficult value to teach a person at any age because society generally promotes instant gratification. However, self-discipline is one of the most important qualities you can help your child develop. Talk with your child about different ways to stay cool when they are angry and to hold off on things that they want to have right now. Role-play how to handle situations at home and school where patience would be helpful.

Play Time!

Choose a Game or Activity to Play for 60 minutes today!

YOU CHOOSE

_____
Write down which game or activity you played today!

Be Healthy!
Listen to your body. If you feel full, it's ok to stop eating!

1
2
3
4
DAY 5
WEEK 4

PARENT TIPS FOR WEEK 5

Skills of the Week

✔ Cause and effect
✔ Electricity
✔ Algebra
✔ Writing a Narrative
✔ Decimals
✔ Reading Comprehension
✔ Fractions
✔ Figurative Language

Weekly Value Kindness

Princess Diana

Kindness is caring about people, animals and the earth. It is looking for ways to help others.

Being nice to others catches on. When people are nice to each other they feel better about themselves and others. Small things make a big difference so when you smile, lend a helping hand and show concern for others; you are making the world a better place.

GET FIT TIME!

Play 60 Every Day!
Run, jump, dance and have fun outside every day for 60 minutes!

Weekly Extension Activities at SummerFitLearning.com

Kindness In Action!
Color the star each day you show kindness through your own actions.

WEEK 5

Color the ⭐ As You Complete Your Daily Task

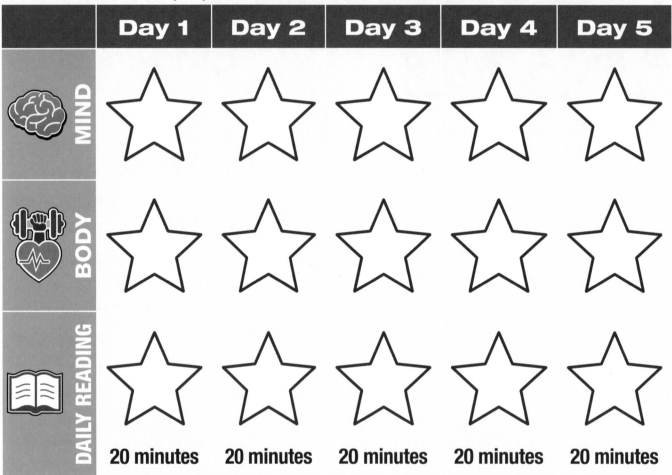

	Day 1	Day 2	Day 3	Day 4	Day 5
MIND	☆	☆	☆	☆	☆
BODY	☆	☆	☆	☆	☆
DAILY READING	☆	☆	☆	☆	☆
	20 minutes	20 minutes	20 minutes	20 minutes	20 minutes

"I am kind"

You can do it!

_____
Print Name

Hardships of Laura Ingalls

Laura Ingalls was born February 7, 1867, seven miles north of the village of Pepin in the "Big Woods" of Wisconsin. She was the second of five children born to Charles and Caroline Ingalls. Living through a difficult time in history, Laura overcame a variety of struggles. Through all of her difficulties, Laura Ingalls managed to become a notable author of children's books. Many children have learned about life on the frontier through her literary contributions.

Laura's family moved many times in a covered wagon in her life. Her father was inspired by the Homestead Act of 1862, which made it possible to acquire 160 acres of land with certain provisions. So he took his family to Independence, Kansas and settled there--an experience that formed the basis of Ingalls' famous novel, *Little House on the Prairie*. The land they settled on was Native American Territory. Not long after settling there, they were forced to move. So in 1871, the family moved back to Wisconsin. Within a few years, her father's restless nature led them on various moves to a claim in Walnut Grove, Minnesota, and the Ingalls lived there with relatives.

Several years later the Ingalls moved once again to the town of De Smet in Dakota Territory. The Ingalls were the first settlers in the town. The following winter (1880-1881) was one of the most severe on record in the Dakotas. While there, the Ingalls attempted again to acquire land through the provisions of the Homestead Act. On December 20, 1882, two months before her 16th birthday, Laura accepted a teaching position, teaching three terms in a one-room school. She later admitted that she did not enjoy teaching, but felt the responsibility to help her family financially. Between 1883-1885, she taught three terms of school, worked for a local dressmaker, and even attended high school although she did not graduate. Her teaching career and her own studies ended when she married Almanzo Wilder, whom she called Manly, on August 25, 1885. In 1886, Charles Ingalls officially had a farm of his own. The settlers of the frontier, including the Ingalls, faced many challenges, including the threat of horrendous weather, starvation, plagues, and sickness.

Directions: Based on the passage above, answer the following questions.

1. Which sentence from the passage shows cause and effect?

A. Many of the settlers had to leave the land they loved due to the one-room school.
B. Laura moved more than once in her life.
C. Later the Ingalls moved to the town of De Smeth in Dakota Territory.
D. The land that they settled on was technically Native American Territory, so not long after they moved there, they were forced to move.

2. Why did Laura not want to continue teaching? _____

_____

3. Of the books that Laura Ingalls wrote which one was her most famous book? _____

_____

WEEK 5

DAY 1

Aerobic

Go to www.summerfitlearning.com for more Activities!

DAILY EXERCISE
Jogging for Fitness 10
"Stretch Before You Play!"

Instruction
Jog 10 minutes in place or outside

Be Healthy!
Wash your fruits and vegetables before eating them.

DAY 1
2
3
4
5
WEEK 5

Physical Science

Basic Electricity

Electricity is a form of energy. It is the flow of electrons along a path. This path is called a "circuit." When a power source, such as a battery or an electrical outlet is used, and is attached to a path (such as a wire or cord), the electrons move along the path rapidly in one direction. This forceful movement causes pressure, which makes it possible to use the energy in some way. For example, to light a lamp the electrons must move very quickly in one direction along the cord (or path). This movement of the electrons creates pressure so that energy is built up. This energy is called "voltage."

Think how this might look in your mind's eye by imagining the electrons are little balls moving through a tube. The tube is like the wire or cord on an electric appliance. The tiny balls that represent electrons in this example are moving quickly, and they continue moving so long as their "path" is complete. This complete path is called a circuit. The wires connect to a battery and then to a light bulb. The battery gives energy to the electrons that are already there in the wire. Once the electrons begin moving they do not stop unless their path is interrupted and the flow cannot happen.

Directions: Answer the questions below.

1. What is the "path" for electricity in a lamp? ______________________________

____

2. Why do the electrons move? ______________________________

____

3. What is meant by a circuit? ______________________________

____

4. What is the pressure called that exists when electrons move along a circuit? ____________

____

5. What purpose does the battery serve in the passage above? ______________

____

Directions: Solve the following equations. Where a variable is written, figure out that value by what is given in the equation. Use mental math.

1. $3 + 4 + 7 =$ _____

2. $4(7 - 3) =$ _____

3. $9 - 4 =$ _____

4. $2(3 + 4) =$ _____

5. $(7 \times 3) + (2 \times 2) =$ _____

6. $(23 - 11) + 7 =$ _____

7. $(30 \div 6) + 4 =$ _____

8. $(6 \times 7) + 8 =$ _____

9. $(10 \div 5) + 4 =$ _____

10. $(123 + 4) =$ _____

11. $(13 + 4) - 7 =$ _____

12. $(14 \div 7) \times 7$ _____

13. $2(90 \div 5) =$ _____

14. $2(3 + 4) =$ _____

15. $(7 \times 7) + 7^2 =$ _____

16. $(28 + 28) \div 2^2 =$ _____

17. $(30 \div 6) + 4 =$ _____

18. $100 - (23 + 9) =$ _____

19. $4(24 - 3) =$ _____

20. $2^2 + 1 =$ _____

21. $(3 \times 3) + 5 =$ _____

22. $(3 - 1) + 8 =$ _____

23. $(6 \div 6) \times 10 =$ _____

24. $(16 - 8) \times 8 =$ _____

25. $8(8 \times 8) =$ _____

26. $18 - 4 =$ _____

27. $5 (3^2) + 6 =$ _____

28. $2 + [2(12 \times 2)] =$ _____

29. $(11 - 5) + 8 =$ _____

30. $(6^2) + 9 =$ _____

Strength
Go to www.summerfitlearning.com for more Activities!

DAILY EXERCISE
Can Do
"Stretch Before You Play!"

Instruction
Repeat 10 times

Be Healthy!
Wash your hands before, during and after cooking food.

 Writing a Narrative

Writing a Narrative

A narrative is a constructive format that describes a sequence of non-fictional or fictional events. For example, you can begin by saying that you made your bed, cleaned your room, ate breakfast, helped clean the kitchen, took your dog for a walk, met some of your neighborhood friends and rode with your mother to the mall--all written in sequential order.

Writing assignment: Write a narrative in which you recount two or more appropriately sequenced events. Include some details regarding what happened. Use some words to signal your order of events. Finally, provide some sense of closure. You may want to use notebook paper first. Either write in the space provided or type your narrative on your computer.

_____

Title

_____
_____
_____
_____
_____
_____
_____
_____
_____
_____
_____
_____
_____
_____
_____

DAY 2

WEEK 5

70 © Summer Fit

Directions: Identify the place value of the underlined digits in section 1 by circling the correct term following each number. In section 2, read each number, then write the new number, the phrase describes.

Section 1	
1. 3.4<u>56</u>	tenths, hundredths, thousandths
2. 45.<u>31</u>	tenths, hundredths, thousandths
3. 5.30<u>1</u>	tenths, hundredths, thousandths
4. .0<u>7</u>	tenths, hundredths, thousandths
5. 6.3<u>7</u>	tenths, hundredths, thousandths
6. 9.<u>5</u>1	tenths, hundredths, thousandths

Section II
7. 13.04, increased *by four tenths* = _____
8. 123.7, lowered *by four* = _____
9. 3.6, increased *by three hundredths* = _____
10. 5.0, reduced *by one tenth* = _____
11. 175.25, increased *by six tenths* = _____
12. 8.001, *lowered by 9 thousandths* = _____

Directions: Compute the following. Rewrite for easier calculation if necessary.

13.	14.	15.	16.
3.4	8.713	19.32	45.337
x 4	+ 12	- 8.07	+ 9.370

17. 79.5 ÷ 5 = _____   **18.** 42.8 ÷ 2 = _____   **19.** 77.05 ÷ 5 = _____   **20.** 85 x 1.2 = _____

Directions: Complete the function boxes using the given rule.

	Rule: + .003	
21.	.8	
22.		.109
23.	7.01	
24.	4.78	
25.	2.4	
26.		7.003
27.	3.4	

	Rule: x .10	
28.	15	
29.		3.0
30.	26	
31.		7.5
32.		900
33.	45	
34.	70	

	Rule: ÷ .25	
35.	125	
36.	75	
37.		801
38.	55.2	
39.	150	
40.		242.1
41.	300.1	

	Rule: - .08	
42.		9.08
43.	10.234	
44.	28.7	
45.		14.52
46.	8.919	
47.	76	
48.	3.08	

Aerobic

Go to www.summerfitlearning.com for more Activities!

DAILY EXERCISE
Green Giant
"Stretch Before You Play!"

Instruction
Ask Mom for 15 minutes of yard work

Be Healthy!
Say "Please" when asking someone to do something for you.

Reading Comprehension

The Jim Crow Laws

Jim Crow laws were enacted in 1876 and mandated through 1965. While the 1863 Emancipation Proclamation offered many new civil liberties to African Americans, many challenges remained for the post-slavery, colored population. The Jim Crow laws were enacted to create a more positive co-existence among races, thus allowing people of different races to live peacefully among one another. However, the wider belief is that the laws became the start of racial segregation. "Separate but equal" was the intent as the ideal would be a life beyond slavery, racial supremacy and blatant discrimination.

Northern states and southern states addressed the laws differently using *de jure* and *de facto* rules for the respective regions. This "separate but equal" stance on human civil rights lasted until the widespread misuse, misunderstanding and intentional discrimination by whites grew to extremes. A group of black men who were lawyers and graduates of Howard University's Law School, cooperated to bring segregation to public awareness so that the Jim Crow laws might be ended due to their unconstitutional nature.

Jim Crow was a fictional black man memorialized in song by demeaning, offensive white musicians, artists and their followers. Naming the laws the Jim Crow laws only added to the mockery of the goal to keep those of different races at "lower places" in white America. Ultimately, these laws were repealed due to their unfair regulations on those of African American, Chinese, Japanese descent. These changes were upheld by the more modern political actions of the southern Civil Rights movement led by Dr. Martin Luther King, Jr.

Directions: Determine if the following statements are true or false according to this passage. Write a T or F in the blank preceding the statement.

______ 1. The purpose of the Jim Crow laws was to end slavery.

______ 2. The Jim Crow laws came after the civil rights movement.

______ 3. Segregation happened as a result of the Jim Crow laws.

______ 4. These laws were only for the people in the southern states.

______ 5. Some lawyers from the north made Jim Crow laws possible.

______ 6. Segregation ended because it was determined as unconstitutional.

Directions: Add or subtract using like denominators.

1. $\dfrac{3}{8}$
    $+ \dfrac{1}{8}$

2. $\dfrac{1}{4}$
    $+ \dfrac{1}{4}$

3. $\dfrac{5}{8}$
    $- \dfrac{2}{8}$

4. $\dfrac{9}{12}$
    $+ \dfrac{3}{12}$

5. $\dfrac{4}{10}$
    $+ \dfrac{3}{10}$

6. $\dfrac{6}{8}$
    $- \dfrac{3}{8}$

7. $\dfrac{2}{5}$
    $+ \dfrac{1}{5}$

8. $\dfrac{4}{9}$
    $+ \dfrac{3}{9}$

9. $\dfrac{14}{15}$
    $- \dfrac{12}{15}$

10. $\dfrac{9}{16}$
    $+ \dfrac{3}{16}$

11. $\dfrac{4}{8}$
    $+ \dfrac{3}{8}$

12. $\dfrac{6}{8}$
    $- \dfrac{3}{8}$

---

13. $\dfrac{1}{8} + \dfrac{2}{8} =$

14. $\dfrac{4}{9} + \dfrac{3}{9} =$

15. $\dfrac{5}{11} + \dfrac{4}{11} =$

16. $\dfrac{5}{16} - \dfrac{4}{16} =$

17. $2\frac{2}{3} + \frac{1}{3} =$ _____

18. $3\frac{5}{8} + 1\frac{7}{8} =$ _____

19. $4\frac{1}{8} - \frac{1}{8} =$ _____

20. $8\frac{1}{3} - 5\frac{1}{3} =$ ___

21. $9\frac{2}{3}$
    $+ \frac{2}{3}$

22. $4\frac{5}{8}$
    $- 3\frac{1}{8}$

23. $14\frac{2}{3}$
    $- 7\frac{1}{3}$

24. $9\frac{1}{2}$
    $- 5\frac{1}{2}$

25. $2\frac{3}{4}$
    $- 1\frac{3}{4}$

Strength

DAILY EXERCISE
Sky Reach
"Stretch Before You Play!"

Instruction
Repeat 10 times, and then switch arms

Be Healthy!
Eat all your meals at the kitchen table today.

Figurative Language

Similes and Metaphors

Figurative language is a tool that an author uses to help the reader visualize what is happening in a story or poem. Some common types of figurative language are as follows: simile, metaphor, alliteration, onomatopoeia, idiom, puns, and sensory language.

A **simile** is a comparison using like or as. Similes usually compare two dissimilar objects. For example: His feet were as big as boats. We are comparing the size of feet to boats.

A **metaphor** states that one thing is something else. It is a comparison, but it does not use like or as to make the comparison. For example: Her hair is silk. The sentence is comparing hair to silk.

Directions: Decide whether each sentence contains a simile or metaphor. Write the word simile if the sentence contains a simile. Write the word metaphor if the sentence contains a metaphor.

_____ 1. Those two silly girls are like two peas in a pod.

_____ 2. No one invites Tony to parties because he's a wet blanket.

_____ 3. The baby boy was like an octopus, grabbing clothes off the racks.

_____ 4. When my brother gets sick, he is a big baby.

_____ 5. When Cesar finished the test, he was white as a ghost.

_____ 6. When we were bathing our dog, the bar of soap was a slippery fish.

_____ 7. Mother declared as she walked in the room, "I feel like a limp dish rag!"

_____ 8. Chris was a wall, bouncing every tennis ball back over the net.

_____ 9. Oscar did not like it when his mother told him his room smelled like an old shoe.

_____10. Be careful using that can opener. It's as temperamental as a chain saw.

© Summer Fit

Kindness is the act or the state of being kind, being marked by good and charitable behavior, pleasant disposition, and concern for others. It is known as a virtue, and recognized as a value in many cultures.

Princess Diana. Diana Frances Spencer was born on July 1, 1961, in Norfolk, England, the third of Lord and Lady Althorp's four children. She grew up next door to the royal family's Sandringham estate. One of Diana's friends was Prince Andrew, Charles' brother. Although Prince Charles had known Diana almost all her life, he thought of her as a friend for his younger brothers. Charles thought Diana was too young to consider as a marriage prospect, and the romance did not bloom for another three years. Reporters began to suspect the nature of her relationship with Charles and began to follow Diana constantly. Charles then proposed to Diana during dinner in Buckingham Palace on February 1981. Diana was the first British citizen to marry the heir to the throne since 1659.

Over the years, Diana became involved in many charitable causes and will always be admired for her kindness and generosity to so many. She called worldwide attention to the problems of homelessness and drug abuse, shook hands with patients at an AIDS ward in a Middlesex hospital, and once visited victims of an Irish Republican Army (IRA) bombing in Northern Ireland. Her royal status was influential in acquiring many resources and money for the sick as well as the poorest sections of the world. Diana's willingness to support such an unglamorous sector of humankind made her a heroine in modern day culture. In 1990, People magazine noted, Diana was involved with forty-four charities, making more than 180 visits on their behalf the previous year. "I don't just want to be a name on a letterhead," the princess was quoted as saying in the Saturday Evening Post. Princess Diana's legacy continues to inspire others to do work from the heart where only kindness is the driving force.

Directions: After reading the passage above, answer the following true-false questions. Write T for True and F for False.

_____ 1. One of Diana's childhood friends was Prince Andrew.

_____ 2. Diana was not the first British citizen to marry the heir to the throne of England.

_____ 3. *People* magazine noted that Diana at one time was involved with forty-four charities.

_____ 4. Diana called attention to the problems of homelessness and drug abuse.

_____ 5. Diana's legacy continues to inspire others to work from the heart where kindness is the driving force.

☐ Make bookmarks out of sayings on kindness like "Kindness can change the world" or "I believe in the magic of kindness." Pass them out to your friends and family.

Core Value Booklist
Read More About Kindness

Have You Filled a Bucket Today
By Carol McCloud

The Kindness of Strangers
By Mike McIntyre

Across Five Aprils
By Irene Hunt

Dude, That's Rude
By Pamela Espeland

Time for Horatio
By Penelope Colville Paine

Reading Extension Activities at SummerFitLearning.com

☐ Random acts of kindness are kind deeds done for someone who is not expecting it. Trace your hand and cut it out. On each finger write a random act of kindness you can do this week.

☐ Start every day with a smile! Smiling is infectious and is an easy way to be kind. Cut out pictures of people smiling from old magazines and make a collage. Have your parents look up the poem "Smiling is Infectious" (author unknown). Try to memorize it and recite it to your family or friends.

Let's Talk About It

Explain what Random Acts of Kindness (RAK) are to your child. Read or tell them a story that incorporates or is based on RAK to help them fully understand the concept. Establish specific days that focus on kindness in different areas of their lives, such as "kindness to your family day," "kindness to the planet day," and "kindness to animals day."

Play Time!
Choose a Game or Activity to Play for 60 minutes today!

YOU CHOOSE

_____
Write down which game or activity you played today!

Be Healthy! Ask your parents if you can do something for them.

1
2
3
4

DAY 5

WEEK 5

PARENT TIPS FOR WEEK 6

Skills of the Week

✔ Verb tense shift
✔ Fractions
✔ Narrative
✔ Computation
✔ Genetics
✔ Ocean Currents
✔ Combining sentences

Weekly Value Courage

Rosa Parks

Courage means doing the right thing even when it is difficult and you are afraid. It means to be brave.

It can be a lot easier to do the right thing when everybody else is doing it, but it can be a lot harder to do it on our own or when nobody is looking. Remember who you are and stand up for what you believe in when it is easy and even more so when it is hard.

GET FIT TIME!

Play 60 Every Day!
Run, jump, dance and have fun outside every day for 60 minutes!

Weekly Extension Activities at SummerFitLearning.com

Courage In Action!
Color the star each day you show Courage through your own actions.

Color the ☆ As You Complete Your Daily Task

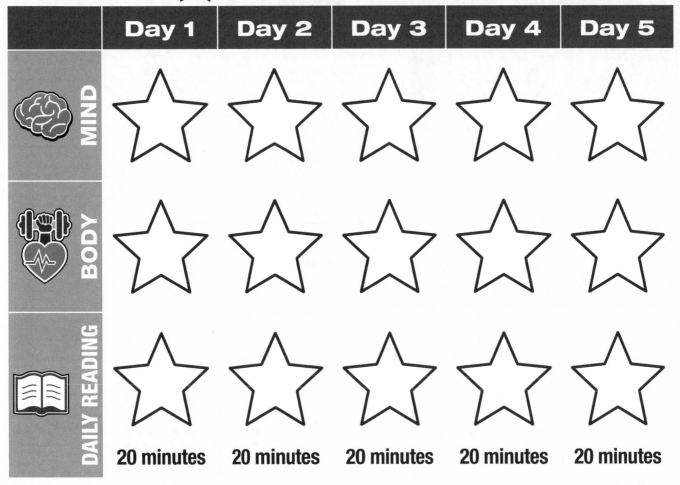

	Day 1	Day 2	Day 3	Day 4	Day 5
MIND	☆	☆	☆	☆	☆
BODY	☆	☆	☆	☆	☆
DAILY READING	☆	☆	☆	☆	☆
	20 minutes	20 minutes	20 minutes	20 minutes	20 minutes

You can do it!

"I am brave"

_____
Print Name

What is Verb Tense Shift?

A **verb tense shift** is easily noted when the writer accidentally "shifts" from present tense to past tense in the passage.

Read the paragraph below and notice the different shifts in verb tense.

Jonathan <u>invited</u> his friend, Nathan, to come over and have dinner with him and his mother. She <u>prepares</u> a big dinner for the three of them, and when they <u>were</u> ready for dessert, she <u>brings</u> a cake out for Jonathan because it was his eleventh birthday. The candles <u>were lit</u>, and the lights <u>are turned</u> out so that he <u>could blow</u> out the candles in the dark. Jonathan's mother then <u>begins</u> to clear the table of the food and dishes.

Observe now how the paragraph reads with the corrected verb tense.

Jonathan invited his friend, Nathan, to come over and have dinner with him and his mother. She prepared a big dinner for the three of them, and when they were ready for dessert, she brought a cake out for Jonathan because it was his eleventh birthday. The candles were lit, and the lights were turned out so that he could blow out the candles in the dark. Jonathan's mother began to clear the table of the food and dishes.

Directions: Some of the verbs are correctly written; others will need to be changed so that the entire selection is written in the **past tense**.

1. David and I realized that we need a change of pace. **2.** After two years of the usual summer job drudgery, it is time for a summer job with pizzazz. **3.** It is David's brilliant idea that we should be camp counselors at Camp Happy Hollow in the mountains of north Georgia. **4.** The first morning at camp we awakened to the sound of a bugle. **5.** I assumed I had just fallen asleep. **6.** 5:00 A.M., apparently, is considered an appropriate rise and shine hour at Camp Happy Hollow. **7.** I am cold, too. **8.** Had I known it is going to be so cold in the north woods, I would have brought more blankets. **9.** After arousing the sleepy campers, we all will march to the dining hall for a hearty breakfast. **10.** Canoeing and swimming lessons will follow breakfast.

DAILY EXERCISE
Capture the Flag
"Stretch Before You Play!"

Instruction
Get Your Family and Friends to Play

Be Healthy!
Water, milk and 100% fruit juice are the best drinks for you!

DAY
1

2 3 4 5

WEEK 6

Fractions

Multiplying & Dividing Fractions

Note: When a product's numerator is larger than the denominator, rewrite the product as a mixed number.

1. $\dfrac{3}{4} \times \dfrac{1}{2} =$ ——

2. $\dfrac{1}{3} \times \dfrac{7}{8} =$ ——

3. $\dfrac{6}{11} \times \dfrac{2}{8} =$ ——

4. $\dfrac{2}{10} \times \dfrac{5}{9} =$ ——

5. $\dfrac{6}{13} \times \dfrac{1}{7} =$ ——

6. $\dfrac{3}{8} \times \dfrac{4}{5} =$ ——

7. $\dfrac{3}{5} \times \dfrac{2}{3} =$ ——

8. $\dfrac{2}{12} \times \dfrac{1}{18} =$ ——

9. $\dfrac{4}{7} \times \dfrac{1}{2} =$ ——

10. $\dfrac{6}{8} \times \dfrac{5}{8} =$ ——

11. $\dfrac{2}{15} \times \dfrac{1}{3} =$ ——

12. $\dfrac{1}{9} \times \dfrac{8}{12} =$ ——

13. $\dfrac{1}{4} \div \dfrac{1}{3} =$ ——

14. $\dfrac{2}{8} \div \dfrac{2}{3} =$ ——

15. $\dfrac{3}{9} \div \dfrac{2}{10} =$ ——

16. $\dfrac{7}{8} \div \dfrac{1}{5} =$ ——

17. When Mary lost her bracelet, it had 12 beads. When she found it, there were only 5 beads on it. What fraction of the beads were lost? What fraction of the beads were still on the bracelet?

Help Wanted: A Book Blogger

Read the announcement above. Imagine **you** received that message from a company wanting **you** to blog for them! What is a blog? A blog is an online diary web page that is updated frequently by the blog owner. It is open to readers via the worldwide web. Bloggers write in the narrative voice, telling about their personal experiences related to a topic. They use words like "I" and "me" because they are telling the story. The most appealing blogs are those with accurate information, useful links to other websites and some good humor.

Use the space below to write your text, illustrations and "featured" blog references. Since you are to blog about books, include writing activity resources such as links to libraries, online dictionaries, and other helpful tools for readers and writers. Make your page super awesome so it will ROCK the blog world! ......Who knows? You may become the most famous "book-blogger" in the world!

Today's Blog Update:	Helpful links to readers and writers:

	This Week's Picture!	The Joke Corner...

Strength

Go to www.summerfitlearning.com for more Activities!

DAILY EXERCISE
Bottle Lift
"Stretch Before You Play!"

Instruction
Repeat 10 times

Be Healthy!
Ask your parents to buy 1% or skim milk instead of whole milk

Computation

Using a Spreadsheet

Directions: Using standard accounting terms (i.e., "debit" for subtraction and "credit" for addition), complete the spreadsheet.

Katherine had the following sequential transactions in her account. The debits and credits are recorded in the chart; some are not. Determine what balances are missing and fill in the missing data. Then answer the questions analyzing Katherine's data.

Item Number	Date	Credit	Debit	Balance
1	12 June	300		300
2	30 June	157.35		457.35
3	1 July		79.81	
4	9 July	10.05		
5	18 July		49.87	
6	27 July		15.5	
7	1 Aug	36.12		
8	4 Aug	200.98		
9	7 Aug		54.81	
10	14 Aug		30	
11	20 Aug	25		

12. What conclusions can you draw from the information on this spreadsheet that describe

Katherine's spending and depositing habits? _____

_____

13. What month did Katherine have the least transactions? Most? _____

_____

14. What is her average daily balance? _____

 **Genetics**

Courage

Genetics Crossword Puzzle

Directions: Solve the puzzle using the across and down clues. Refer to the "word bank" for the vocabulary words. Be sure to choose the best term.

Word Bank:
parent
offspring
eye color
DNA
trait
gene
chromosome
organisms
heredity
environment
behavior
learned behavior
expressed
half

Across
1. DNA structure containing genes
3. Amount of genetic information each parent gives
7. Function of operating of an offspring after being taught
10. Genetic structures of cellular organisms
11. Living things
12. Found in chromosomes; these transmit and express traits

Down
2. A child; a product of reproductive processes
3. Transmission of traits to offspring
4. A distinguishing inherited characteristic
5. The ancestor of an offspring
6. How an organism naturally functions or operates
8. Non-genetic influences
9. Facial trait in humans that is a result of their genes
13. Evidence of a gene's presence

DAY 3

WEEK 6

Aerobic
Go to www.summerfitlearning.com for more Activities!

DAILY EXERCISE
Happy Feet
"Stretch Before You Play!"

Instruction
Ask your parents to walk with you after dinner

Be Healthy!
Ask mom and dad to play with you!

Ocean Currents

When speaking of water, the word current refers to the motion of the water. Currents are found in many bodies of water – rivers, ponds, even swimming pools. But the currents in the ocean are more complex. These currents may be influenced by tides or winds.

Knowing about currents helps fishermen and the shipping industry. When crossing the ocean in a ship powered by the wind (via sails), being carried by an ocean current (or avoiding a current going the opposite direction) could save a ship more than a week of travel time. Modern ships are powerful enough to go against most ocean currents, but doing so costs time and fuel (e.g., oil = money), so knowledge of ocean currents is still very important.

Ocean currents are also studied because they carry things in the water from place to place in the ocean, like ocean pollution. Knowledge of the local ocean currents can help us determine where sewage is leaking into the ocean or predict how far away the pollution from a leaking sewage pipe will affect the shoreline. Oil companies need to study ocean currents to prepare emergency plans in case an oil spill occurs. Ocean currents also carry warm and cold water from place to place, and can have a significant impact on a region's climate (e.g., the east and west coasts of the United States are quite different).

Try this activity. Fill a tin pie plate to the inner rim with cold tap water. Sprinkle a teaspoon of herb (oregano or chili powder) over the surface. Using a plastic or paper straw, gently blow across the middle of the surface from one side of the pan. The wind you are creating is like the Equatorial Currents flowing west at the Earth's equator. These currents move in a clockwise rotation in the Northern Hemisphere and a counterclockwise rotation in the Southern Hemisphere because of the Earth's rotation and the landmasses that obstruct the waters' flow. Write a sentence to describe the patterns created by the motion of the herbs.

_____

_____

_____

_____

_____

_____

Directions: Simplify the following fractions to lowest terms.

1. 9/12 = _____

2. 3/15 = _____

3. 5/10 = _____

4. 2/8 = _____

5. 16/4 = _____

6. 8/56 = _____

7. 35/20 = _____

8. 7/21 = _____

9. 14/84 = _____

10. 12/2 = _____

11. 3/18 = _____

12. 6/15 = _____

13. 80/12 = _____

14. 13/3 = _____

15. 5/100 = _____

16. 20/ 30 = _____

Prepositional Phrases

Remember that a prepositional phrase is composed of a preposition, the object of the preposition, and all the words (modifiers) in between.

Directions: Underline each **prepositional phrase once**.

17. On Tuesday of next week my mother has an appointment with her dentist.

18. During the press conference, Atlanta's mayor talked about the many traffic problems.

19. The members of the softball team want t-shirts with the club emblem.

20. During the concert at the park, two pigeons got inside the concession area.

21. Under my father's desk is where you will probably find my brother's tennis shoes.

22. Mrs. Moore required her students to memorize the state capitals within three months.

23. Two young boys were ready to begin their trip from Atlanta to Savannah, Georgia.

24. A picnic basket of food and a jug of lemonade were placed inside the car.

25. Between 1830 and 1860, the Underground Railroad brought about 50,000 slaves to freedom.

26. Margie worked extremely hard on her thesis and hoped it would be published soon.

DAY 4

WEEK 6

DAILY EXERCISE
Chop n Squat
"Stretch Before You Play!"

Instruction
Repeat 10 times

Be Healthy!
Drinking soda can give you cavities and add unhealthy fat to your body.

Combining Sentences

Writers can join two short, choppy sentences into one that is more interesting. To combine two short, choppy sentences into a compound sentence, use a comma and a conjunction. Use the conjunction **and** to join two sentences that show addition or similarity. Use the conjunction **but** to join two sentences that show contrast. Use the conjunction **or** to join two sentences that show choice.

Examples: Jessica purchased a new computer. She likes it very much.

Jessica purchased a new computer, and she likes it very much.

Corey ran up the stairs. He stopped at the bedroom.

Corey ran up the stairs, but he stopped at the bedroom.

Should Randy go inside? Should Randy explore outside?

Should Randy go inside, or should he explore outside?

Directions: Using a conjunction and punctuation, combine the simple sentences into one compound sentence.

1. Anthony can play the drums. He can play the guitar.

_____

2. Mary Alice pushed the button. The old bookcase moved.

_____

3. Muhammad Ali was a boxer who never wanted to quit. Ali has Parkinson's disease.

_____

4. Ginger went to work. She did not want to go.

_____

5. That movie looks great I would love to come see it with you.

_____

Courage is the state or quality of mind or spirit that enables one to face danger, fear, or with confidence, and resolution. Courage includes being brave.

Rosa Parks. When Rosa Parks was growing up, African Americans paid the same ten-cent bus fare as whites. However, in many Southern towns, Jim Crow laws said that African Americans had to sit in the back of the bus. These laws also stated that if the "whites only" section was full, African Americans had to give their seats to white riders. A few stops after Rosa sat down, a white passenger got on the bus. When the bus driver noticed that a white person was standing, he called back to the four black people and told them to give up their seats.

The other three got up and stood at the back of the bus. Rosa Parks, who had put in a long day's work as a seamstress, was the first one to say no. On this day Rosa stood up for what she believed in and what was right. She said it in a way that gave others in the South the courage to say no, too.

The police in Montgomery, Alabama were called and Rosa was arrested on December 1, 1955. Black leaders decided to make their stand. Everyone who knew Rosa Parks respected her kind, gentle manner. While the black community fought for change by boycotting city buses, lawyers battled in courts. The bus boycott ended December 20, 1956, when the U.S. Supreme Court ruled that segregation of Montgomery's buses violated the Constitution of the U.S.

DAY 5

Directions: After reading Rosa Parks' passage, fill in the blanks to the questions.

1. In many Southern towns, _____ _____ laws said that African Americans had to sit in the back of the bus.

2. A few stops after Rosa sat down, a white passenger got on the bus. When the bus driver noticed that a white person was standing, he called back to the _____ black people and told them to _____ up their seats.

3. When Rosa lived in Montgomery, Alabama, she worked as a _____.

4. Rosa would not give up her seat on the bus because she felt that it was not _____.

5. The bus boycott ended _____ when the U.S. Supreme Court ruled that segregation of Montgomery's buses violated the U.S. Constitution.

☐ Think of five situations in your everyday life when you might need courage. Think about how you can choose to be brave and then role-play the situations with your family.

Core Value Booklist
Read More About Courage

The Courage of Sarah Noble
By Alice DagResh

A Night to Remember
By Walter Lord

Stone Fox
By John Reynolds Gardner

Call It Courage
By Armstrong Sperry

The Sign of the Beaver
By Elizabeth George Speare

Reading Extension
Activities at
SummerFitLearning.com

☐ Write a letter to a brave person in your community (for instance, a firefighter, police officer, or soldier). Thank them for their bravery.

☐ Come up with a motto for yourself or your family, like "The courage to be brave." Or "Stand up, stand tall, stand brave." Design and color a shield to represent your motto. Remember your motto when facing something that requires your courage.

☐ Talk to your parents about bullying. Do you know any bullies? Are you a bully? How can you show courage and stand up against bullying?

Let's Talk About It

Encourage your children to be the best they can be. Praise them when you see them being brave or showing courage. Talk about and role-play opportunities that arise each day in which they can be courageous.

Play Time!
Choose a Game or Activity to Play for 60 minutes today!

YOU CHOOSE

Write down which game or activity you played today!

Be Healthy!
Try to eat 3 different vegetables today!

DAY 5

WEEK 6

WEEK 7

PARENT TIPS FOR WEEK 7

Skills of the Week

✔ Reading Comprehension
✔ Pollution
✔ Measurement
✔ Homophones
✔ U.S. History
✔ Poetry Interpretation
✔ Greek root words

Weekly Value Respect

Respect is honoring yourself and others. It is behaving in a way that makes life peaceful and orderly.

Mahatma Gandhi

Sometimes we forget to appreciate that every person is unique and different. All of us want to be accepted and appreciated for who we are. Try to treat others the way that you want to be treated, even when it is difficult.

GET FIT TIME!

Play 60 Every Day!
Run, jump, dance and have fun outside every day for 60 minutes!

Weekly Extension Activities at SummerFitLearning.com

Respect In Action!
Color the star each day you show respect through your own actions.

WEEK 7

Color the ⭐ As You Complete Your Daily Task

	Day 1	Day 2	Day 3	Day 4	Day 5
MIND	☆	☆	☆	☆	☆
BODY	☆	☆	☆	☆	☆
DAILY READING	☆	☆	☆	☆	☆
	20 minutes	20 minutes	20 minutes	20 minutes	20 minutes

You can do it!

"I am respectful"

Print Name

Respect

This black lab is not the dog in the story

DAY 1

3

4

5

WEEK 7

Sabi a sniffer dog who went missing in action after a battle in Afghanistan has miraculously been found safe and sound after more than a year in the desert. The black Labrador is said to have been with a joint Australian-Afghan army patrol when it was ambushed by Taliban militants in September 2008. Nine soldiers were wounded during the skirmish that followed, and when the dust settled, there was no sign of the bomb-sniffing dog, who had been trained by U.S. military in October 2007.

Then, in November 2009, 14 months after she disappeared, a U.S. serviceman spotted a dog that appeared to be military trained with an Afghan man at an isolated patrol base. Within days, the lost lab was returned to her unit. The prized pooch came home to roost just in time for a visit by Prime Minister Kevin Rudd. She was described as "composed and relaxed" and no worse for wear after her desert adventures.

Exactly what happened to Sabi and how she spent her days during her 14 month disappearance is unknown, but her good condition and happy disposition shows she was well loved and cared for. (But, of course, conspiracy theorists are already suggesting that she is a spy.) Sabi is just one of many dogs in Afghanistan trained to sniff out roadside bombs and other hidden explosives.

Directions: Choose the best answer for the following multiple choice questions.

1. The actual title of this true story is not given on this page. What do you think is the real title?
   A. Sabi, a Sniffer Dog
   B. Nine Soldiers Wounded
   C. Labrador Reappears after 14 Months
   D. The Lost Lab Returned to Her Unit

2. A U.S. serviceman spotted Sabi after she had been missing since . . .
   A. October 2007.
   B. September 2008.
   C. November 2009.
   D. October 2008.

3. Sabi came home just in time for a visit from
   A. the nine soldiers that were wounded.
   B. the Prime Minister Kevin Rudd.
   C. an Afgan man at an isolated patrol base.
   D. U.S. servicemen who were leaving.

Aerobic

DAILY EXERCISE
Let's Roll
"Stretch Before You Play!"

Instruction
Ride for 10 Minutes

Be Healthy!
Do not interrupt when someone is talking to you.

DAY 1

Pollution

Natural disasters keep scientists very busy. Studying the many changes these events cause the planet help uncover many mysteries that still exist as well as aid in predicting future occurrences of the same or perhaps new ones. However, what is not new to our planet is something more of a "human disaster." This disaster is pollution. Pollution could be lessened if not completely avoided with a little more human effort. Living on this planet requires more and more careful, thoughtful conservation as a means to protect what resources we have. Air, water, soil, vegetation and other resources are negatively impacted by thoughtless overuse of materials, unnecessary waste and improperly managed resources. Merely taking small but effective measures to control our pollution habits, we can help prevent many future problems for younger generations.

Public service announcements to "go green," "reduce, reuse & recycle" are seen practically everywhere from bumper stickers to grocery bags. We read them, hear them and even say them to others, but often do not heed them. For example, an enormous reduction in plastic waste would happen if people consistently used reusable, cloth bags for groceries. Recycling plastic beverage bottles or replacing their use with washable sports bottles would help our landfills dramatically. Even paper waste would be reduced if cloth napkins and dishtowels were substituted for paper towels and napkins. Changes that would reduce or eliminate pollution are positive and not that hard to do once the routine becomes a habit.

Directions: Read each statement. Indicate if it is true or false by writing T or F in the preceding blank. Multimedia Exercise: On separate paper or a computer, create an illustration that could remind people of ways to practice helpful routines.

_____ 1. Pollution is caused by natural disasters.

_____ 2. Reduce, reuse and recycle is a popular slogan to encourage people to change habits.

_____ 3. Small changes people make daily do not significantly help pollution problems.

_____ 4. Humans cause most of the pollution problems on earth but don't seem to create new habits.

_____ 5. Using more cloth products in lieu of paper is a way to reduce pollution.

_____ 6. Factories cause pollution but were not mentioned in this passage.

WEEK 7

Directions: Convert the following measurements using English and metric units of measurements. Read each item thoroughly to ensure the proper unit of conversion. Refer to the chart as needed.

Length Conversion Table						
Metric Units					English Units	
Kilometers	**Meters**	**Millimeters**	**Inches**	**Feet**	**Yards**	**Miles**
1	1,000	1,000,000	39,370	3,281	1,094	0.6214
0.001	1	1,000	39.37	3.281	1.094	0.0006214

1. 4 m = _____ yds.   2. 100 inches = _____ mm   3. 30 km = ____ miles   4. 12 in = _____ ft.

5. 50 km = _____ m   6. 18 inches = _____ mm   7. 8 km = _____ meters   8. 120 in = _____ ft.

9. 10 in. = _____ mm   10. 3 km = _____ miles   11. 144 in = _____ ft.   12. 1000 meters = ____ km

Volume Conversion Table (Liquid Measure)				
Metric Units		U.S. Liquid Measure Units		
Liters	**Milliliters**	**Fluid Ounces**	**Quarts**	**Gallons**
1	1,000	33.81	1.057	0.2642
0.001	1	0.03381	0.001057	0.0002642

13. 1 liter = _____ ml   14. 100 ml = _____ oz.   15. 21.76 oz = _____ gal   16. 9 gal. = _____ qts.

17. 50 oz. = _____ qt.   18. 4 qt. = _____ gal.   19. 18 gal = _____ qt.   20. 85 gal. = _____ l

21. 4ml = _____ oz.   22. 64 oz = _____ gal.   23. 500 l = _____ qts.   24. 12 l = _____ ml.

Multimedia Activity: Go to an on-line song list or movie list on your computer. List the movies or songs by duration from least to greatest. Choose at least four. Then create a playlist of the media from shortest to the longest.

DAILY EXERCISE
Side Step
"Stretch Before You Play!"

Instruction
Repeat 5 times in each direction

Be Healthy!
Instead of eating white potatoes, try sweet potatoes!

Homophones

Homophones are words that have the same pronunciation, but different spelling and different meanings.

Directions: Underline the correct homophone in each sentence.

1. My grandfather does not want to talk about the (passed, past) anymore.

2. Joshua is going to (ware, wear) his new jeans to the party tonight.

3. "Mother, may I please go (to, too, two) the birthday party?"

4. The flight attendant walked down the (aisle, isle) of the plane.

5. Please try not to (waste, waist) computer paper.

6. Isabelle (new, knew) everyone on her swimming team.

7. Jeff and Carmen invited me to come to (there, their) new house for dessert.

8. You can (by, buy) a great used computer at Moore's Supplies and Computers.

9. Christopher likes to (read, reed) books and magazines about sports.

10. Aunt Margaret saw a restaurant just off the (rode, road) about a mile from the mall.

11. Would you please (clothes, close) the door to the basement?

12. We need to take a (break, brake) from these exercises.

The Bill of Rights

On September 25, 1789 twelve amendments to the US Constitution were proposed to the states as amendments to the Constitution in an effort to further define citizens' rights under the newly established government. Congress ratified the items on December 15, 1791, choosing only ten of the twelve proposed amendments. These were called The Bill of Rights and provided clearer parameters on the assertions of the Constitution in plainer, exacting language. Over the years legislators have found loopholes and inconsistencies in the Constitution as life and law coexist in what is hoped for the betterment of mankind. The following charts outline the amendments and their respective topics.

Directions: Using information from the charts and the paragraph, answer the following questions in the space provided. Form your answers in complete, thorough sentences.

The First Ten Bill of Rights:	Later Amendments
Amendment 1 Freedoms, Petitions, Assembly	Amendment 11 Lawsuits against states
Amendment 2 Right to bear arms	Amendment 12 Presidential elections
Amendment 3 Quartering of soldiers	Amendment 13 Abolition of slavery
Amendment 4 Search and arrest	Amendment 14 Civil rights
Amendment 5 Rights in criminal cases	Amendment 15 Black suffrage
Amendment 6 Right to a fair trial	Amendment 16 Income taxes
Amendment 7 Rights in civil cases	Amendment 17 Senatorial elections
Amendment 8 Bail, fines, punishment	Amendment 18 Prohibition of liquor
Amendment 9 Rights retained by the People	Amendment 19 Women's suffrage
Amendment 10 States' rights	Amendment 20 Terms of office
	Amendment 21 Repeal of Prohibition
	Amendment 22 Term Limits for the Presidency
	Amendment 23 Washington, D.C., suffrage
	Amendment 24 Abolition of poll taxes
	Amendment 25 Presidential succession
	Amendment 26 18-year-old suffrage
	Amendment 27 Congressional pay raises

1. Why were only ten of the twelve amendments ratified in 1791? _____
_____

2. Considering the list of amendments, how many appear to address issues related to elected officials, and what are those? _____

3. Which of the Bill of Rights is specifically for people accused of a crime? _____

4. Because amendment 25 relates to "Presidential Succession," what would that most likely include, generally speaking? _____
_____

5. How is the Constitution impacted by these amendments, then and now? _____
_____
_____

DAY
3

WEEK 7

Aerobic
Go to www.summerfitlearning.com for more Activities!

DAILY EXERCISE
Speed
"Stretch Before You Play!"

Instruction
Run 2 Blocks

Be Healthy!
Drive by the drive-thru: it's hard to get healthy fast food!

1

DAY 3

5

WEEK 7

 Interpreting Poetry and Mood

I Choose

I choose to be nice and help out in life;
I choose to be happy, and smile all I can.
I chose my friends, and they chose me back!
I like my life and all that it brings;
But mostly I choose people before things.

Thursday

Last Thursday was like blackness, thunder and gray.
I was glad to go to bed; sleep will make Thursday go quickly away.
I hate bad days where such sadness is real,
If only he knew how he made my heart feel.
If I see him years later, by an unfortunate chance,
I hope it's a Thursday, since he ruined that dance.

Directions: After reading each poem, answer the questions below that compare and contrast the two.

1. What is the mood of the first poem?
   a) sadness   b) happiness
   c) revenge   d) excitement

2. What is the mood of the second poem?
   a) sadness   b) happiness
   c) revenge   d) excitement

3. In the poem "Thursday" who is "him"?
   a) boyfriend   b) brother
   c) dad   d) unknown

4. What is the obvious difference in the two poems?
   a) They are each most likely written by very different aged authors.
   b) They are each about an experience at school or a school event.
   c) They are each about very different emotions teenagers have.
   d) They are each poems where the writer is complaining about something.

5. What similarities are most obvious to the reader?
   a) They both have a lot of sad emotions and seem like the author does not have friends.
   b) They both are written about things kids and teens think about and are the same age.
   c) They are both about school and school dances.
   d) They are both about adolescents who have favorite pets.

In our everyday lives, we use Greek root words and definitions all the time. We may not always notice these root words as well as their definitions because we are so accustomed to their being a normal part of our lives. Many words that we use stem from a Greek word and are very common in our language.

All of the following are common Greek root words and their definitions. At some point in your life, you may have or will use these root words to make up a full word for a paper or possibly in conversation.

```
Α Β Γ Δ Ε
Ζ Η Θ Ι Κ
Λ Μ Ν Ξ Ο
Π Ρ Σ Τ Υ
Φ Χ Ψ Ω
```

Auto - referring to the self
Biblio - anything pertaining to a book
Bios - life or living things in general
Cosmos - order or world
Demos - pertaining people
Derma - referring to skin
Geo - pertaining to the earth
Hydro - pertaining to water
Hypno - pertaining to sleep
Kilo - thousand

Mania - pertaining to madness
Mega - large or powerful
Monos - pertaining to one
Octo - eight
Phobia - fear or dread of something
Pyscho - pertaining to the soul or mind
Tele - referring to something far off
Therapy - pertaining to curing
Thermo - pertaining to heat
Thesis - a position or opinion

Directions: Since you have been exposed to some of the Greek root words and their definitions, you should have no problem using and understanding words composed from them in everyday conversation. The following sentences use some of the words with Greek roots. <u>Underline</u> those words that are composed with a Greek root.

1. Manuel is claustrophobic when he steps into an elevator.

2. Our home thermostat registered over 100 degrees yesterday.

3. Natasha had to finish her bibliography for her science research paper.

4. Aunt Maurene went to the dermatologist because she had several red spots on her face.

5. My Uncle Thomas, an astronomer, studies stars and planets.

6. All the children in kindergarten were tested for autoimmune disorders.

7. Diego received a new telescope for his eleventh birthday.

8. My father has a degree in clinical psychology.

DAY
4

WEEK 7

Strength
Go to www.summerfitlearning.com for more Activities!

DAILY EXERCISE
Balance
"Stretch Before You Play!"

Instruction
Hold each for 15 seconds, then switch legs and repeat

Be Healthy!
Make a card for someone in your family today.

American History

America's Forgotten War

The War of 1812 has been called "America's forgotten war." Many historians argue that the war was a complete waste of resources and lives. The war was fought between the Revolution and the Civil War. In 1808, Britain and France were at war. The U.S. did not take either side, but Britain and the U.S. became enemies. British officers raided American ships to look for British sailors on the ships. American sailors were caught and forced to serve in the British Navy, which was called impressment. The U.S. government was extremely angry about impressment. It was also angry that the British were helping Indians fight Western settlers.

Thus in 1812, the U.S. declared war on Britain. Americans wanted to stop impressment. They also wanted Britain to stop arming the Indians. The war was primarily fought on the Great Lakes and in the Atlantic Ocean. In 1814, the British navy fired at Fort McHenry. Francis Scott Key watched the battle. He saw the American flag flying above the fort and wrote "The Star-Spangled Banner," which became the national anthem.

After three years of fighting and nearly 6,000 casualties, the U.S. and Great Britain agreed to a treaty that really did not resolve any of the issues that prompted the war. Unaware of the treaty, British forces attacked Americans in New Orleans. The British were defeated. The war ended March 23, 1815. In fact, the argument over trade policies that had preceded the war continued well into the 1820's, almost as though the war had never occurred at all.

Directions: Answer the following questions based on the passage above.

1. The War of 1812 was wedged between what two wars? _____

2. One group of historians argues that the war was a complete _____.

3. The war was primarily fought on the _____ and in the _____.

4. After _____ years of fighting and nearly _____ casualties, the U.S. and Great Britain agreed to a treaty.

Respect gives a positive feeling of esteem for a person or other entity (such as a nation), and also specific actions and conduct representative of that esteem. Respect can be a specific feeling of regard for the actual qualities of the one respected.

Mahatma Gandi. Mahatma Gandi was born in Porbandar, India on October 2, 1869. His father was a prime minister in the prince's court. His mother was a devout woman who taught her children about their religion, Jainism. Gandhi grew up believing in karma—the idea that to keep a soul clean, one should pray, be disciplined, honest, have few possessions, and respect everyone.

In all respects, Gandhi was an uncommon person. Outraged by human suffering, revolted by injustice, and guided by faith, Gandhi spent his life in India and Africa standing up for what he believed to be right. He did this with unfailing strength, ready to give his life for the poorest and most despised in the belief that every human being should be able to live with dignity and freedom.

Gandhi helped India gain independence by using non-violent means and is considered to be "The Father of the Nation." On the evening of January 30, 1948, as Gandhi walked to a prayer meeting, where thousands of people awaited him, a Hindu man named Nathuram Godse fired a gun at his heart. Gandhi fell. His last words were those of compassion and love: "I forgive you, I love you, I bless you."

Directions: Fill in the blanks using words from the passage above.

1. In all respects, Gandhi was an _____ person.

2. Gandhi spent most of his life in _____ and _____ standing up for what he believed to be right.

3. Gandhi helped India gain independence and is considered to be

"_____."

4. He grew up believing in karma--the idea that to keep a soul clean, one should _____,

be _____, _____, have few _____, and _____

everyone.

5. Gandhi's life ended when he was _____ on the way to a prayer meeting, where thousands awaited him.

☐ Cut out pictures from old magazines to make a collage of what **RESPECT** looks like. Include examples of respecting self, others, property, and the environment.

☐ Write out the word respect vertically on a piece of paper. Think of a word that means respect for each letter (R = responsibility, E = equality).

☐ Design a bumper sticker about respect. Use the word **RESPECT** and add at least 3 qualities to your bumper sticker.

Core Value Booklist
Read More About Respect

The Pearl
By John Steinbeck

Steal Away Home
By Lois Ruby

Code Talker: A Novel About the Navajo Marines
By Joseph Brunchac

Rosa Parks: My Story
By Rosa Parks

The Phantom Tollbooth
By Norton Juster

Reading Extension Activities at SummerFitLearning.com

Let's Talk About It

The best way you can teach respect is by showing respect to others and yourself. When a child sees and feels respect, he/she begins to understand how important it is. Schools teach respect, but parents have the most influence on how respectful children become. Talk with your child about respect at home and at school.

Stepping Stones

Stepping Stones Entertainment™ was founded by parents who wanted to provide meaningful family movies to help inspire common values. It is composed of people from many different backgrounds, nationalities, and beliefs. For more than 20 years, Stepping Stones has provided families with movies about integrity, charity, forgiveness, and many other common values through hundreds of films for all ages. Learn more at **www.steppingstones.com**.

STEPPING STONES.COM
Meaningful Family Movies

Play Time!
Choose a Game or Activity to Play for 60 minutes today!

YOU CHOOSE

Write down which game or activity you played today!

Be Healthy!
Clean the kitchen without being asked.

WEEK 7

DAY 5

1
2
3

WEEK 8

Skills of the Week

- ✔ Punctuating parenthetical expressions
- ✔ Ratios and Percent
- ✔ Informative Writing
- ✔ Geography of Modern Europe
- ✔ Earth science - Soil Horizons
- ✔ Possessive Personal Pronouns
- ✔ Incredible Equations
- ✔ Government Forms: Home and School
- ✔ Creating an Outline

Weekly Value Responsibility

Being responsible means others can depend on you. It is being accountable for what you do and for what you do not do.

Terry Fox

A lot of times it is easier to look to someone else to step forward and do the work or to blame others when it does not get done. You are smart, capable and able so try to be the person who accepts challenges and does not blame others if it does not get done.

GET FIT TIME!

Play 60 Every Day!

Run, jump, dance and have fun outside every day for 60 minutes!

Weekly Extension Activities at SummerFitLearning.com

Responsibility In Action!

Color the star each day you show responsibility through your own actions.

WEEK 8
HEALTHY MIND + HEALTHY BODY

Color the ⭐ As You Complete Your Daily Task

	Day 1	Day 2	Day 3	Day 4	Day 5
MIND	⭐	⭐	⭐	⭐	⭐
BODY	⭐	⭐	⭐	⭐	⭐
DAILY READING	⭐ 20 minutes	⭐ 20 minutes	⭐ 20 minutes	⭐ 20 minutes	⭐ 20 minutes

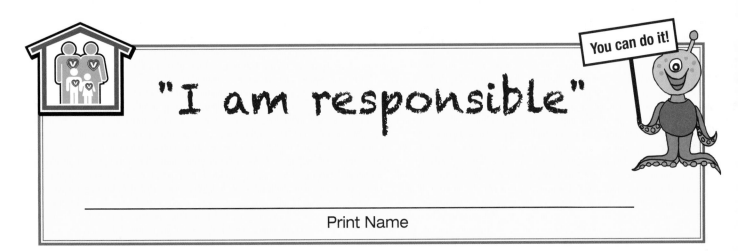

You can do it!

"I am responsible"

_____
Print Name

Punctuating Parenthetical Expressions

Responsibility

Expressions that are not really part of the main idea of the sentence, or that interrupt the main sentence, are known as **parenthetical**. When spoken, such expressions are indicated by a pause before and after the expression. In writing, these pauses are indicated with commas, dashes, or parentheses. For example: I believe (think, know, hope), I am sure, on the contrary, on the other hand, by the way, in my opinion, in fact, to tell the truth, however, for example, nevertheless.

Directions: Punctuate the following parenthetical expressions.

1. The members of the board therefore agreed to sign the petition.

2. These same council members you may recall voted themselves a 35 percent pay increase last year.

3. Indeed you have found a great piece of art.

4. This equivalent ratio rule is in fact extremely important.

5. The moral of the story is that people should always as a result treat one another with kindness.

Ratio and Percent

Remember that a **ratio** is a way of comparing numbers. When a number is part of 100, the ratio is called a **percent**. Circle the correct answer in the following questions.

6. Change 9/25 to a percent.

    A. 25%   B. 9%

    C. 36%   D. 45%

7. Which is the ratio of 8:6 written as a fraction that has been reduced to lowest terms?

    A. 6/8   B. 8/6

    C. 3/4   D. 1 1/3

8. Which fraction expresses the ratio of 28 students to 1 teacher?

    A. 28/28   B. 28/1

    C. 28/28   D. 1/28

9. Tanya received an 80% score on her science test. What fraction of the questions did she answer correctly?

    A. 4/5   B. 3/5

    C. 2/5   D. 1/5

10. Zackry invited 32 of his friends to his birthday party. If 24 friends attended, what percent of friends attended?

    A. 65%   B. 75%

    C. 80%   D. 85%

DAY 1

WEEK 8

Aerobic

DAILY EXERCISE
Hopscotch
"Stretch Before You Play!"

Instruction
Play 3 Games

Be Healthy!
A good night's sleep is important for everybody!

DAY 1

WEEK 8

 Informative Writing

A very large track of land is being sold in your city. Fictitious bidders include a cancer research hospital, a shopping-mall developer, a large car dealership, and a well-known gas/convenience store. Choose one and become a activist for one of the developers, writing arguments and/or explantations on behalf of their interests. Carefully develop your topic with relevant facts, details, quotations from other sources, and other necessary information and examples. Use the space below to develop your information and then use your computer to type the final paper.

_____

_____

_____

_____

_____

_____

_____

_____

_____

_____

Geography of Modern Europe

Directions: Complete the criss-cross puzzle using 12 geographic terms related to modern Europe. Use a modern political map of Europe for reference from a book, atlas or a credible online resource.

DAY
2

5

WEEK 8

Across:

1. Shares a large border with France and is north of Italy.

5. Surrounded by the Atlantic Ocean, east of Ireland and north of France

6. Borders Mediterranean Sea and south of France

8. The ocean east of the U.K. and France

11. Cardinal direction opposite of north

Down:

2. Largest landmass of the European countries, east of Finland & Ukraine

3. Shaped like a boot and is surrounded by the Mediterranean Sea

4. Large border of Atlantic Ocean coastline, borders Italy on the southeast and Germany to the northeast

5. Black Sea is at its South; this country is bordered by Romania & Russia.

7. Nestled between France's northern border and Germany's western border

9. Cardinal direction opposite of south

10. South of Baltic Sea, east of Germany and west of Russia

DAILY EXERCISE
Toe Taps
"Stretch Before You Play!"

Instruction
Repeat 10 times
with each foot

DAY 2

4

5

WEEK 8

 Earth Science - Soil Horizons

Directions: Below is a list of clues that describe different layers or horizon of earth's soil that is being described.

O Horizon – The top, organic layer of soil, humus.

A Horizon – Topsoil: made of humus & mineral particles. Below O & above E, dark in color & allows seeds to germinate.

E Horizon – This is beneath A, B & contains mostly sand, silt and very few minerals due to elevation.

B Horizon – Beneath E, above R; this horizon is mostly broken bedrock, not penetrable by plants.

R Horizon – The bottom layer, untouched by weathering; bedrock.

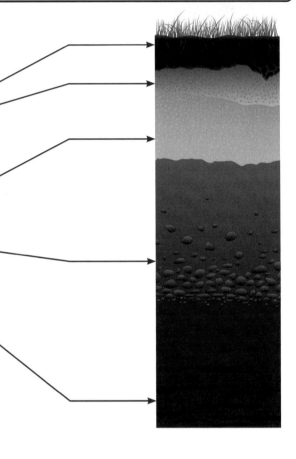

Directions: Read the following statements that other students wrote. Decide what is incorrect about the way they drew conclusions about the diagram. Rewrite what they wrote so that it is grammatically correct and factual.

1. Plants grow best on all of the horizons except R.

_____

2. Seeds need to germinate on layers that have the most broken rock.

_____

3. Studying the soil layers is a way of looking at changes to only horizons A & O.

_____

4. Each horizon is not similar to the horizon above or below it because of their vast differences.

_____

5. Horizons E, B, and R are most conducive to growing plants and weathering.

_____

Possessive personal pronouns do not require an apostrophe. Possessive personal pronouns are as follows: my, mine, your, yours, his, her, hers, its, our, ours, their, theirs. They are used before a noun. Do not write it's (meaning "it is") for its or they're (meaning "they are") for their.

Directions: Underline the correct form of the possessive pronoun in parentheses.

1. (Their, They're) schedule calls for a seminar on Tuesday and Wednesday of this week.
2. When I first read her book, I was surprised by the quality of (its, it's) artwork.
3. The students (who's whose) names are called are to report to the auditorium.
4. "The trophy is (ours, ours')!" shouted the captain of the soccer team.
5. (Hers, Hers') is the red bicycle with the reflectors on (its, it's) fenders.
6. Arlene, the two poems of (yours, yours') have been selected for the Atlanta Magazine.

Incredible Equations

Directions: Use the following numbers to make 5 "incredible equations." The target number is given and there is space for you to write 5 equations that equal the target number. Be sure to include the = sign, so that it is a real "equation" and not just an expression. Make your equations truly INCREDIBLE by making them increasingly difficult. An example is done for you using the target number of 45.

Example: Target number 45

1. $9 \times 5 = 45$ 2. $90/2 = 45$ 3. $(25/5) \times 9 = 45$ 4. $(5^2) + 20 = 45$ 5. $(\frac{1}{2} \times 100) - 5 = 45$

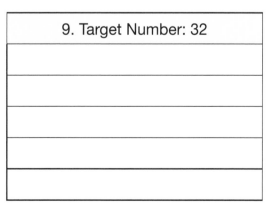

7. Target Number: 60

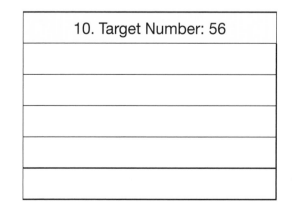

8. Target Number: 84

9. Target Number: 32

10. Target Number: 56

Aerobic Go to www.summerfitlearning.com for more Activities!

DAILY EXERCISE
Tag
"Stretch Before You Play!"

Instruction
Get your family and friends to play

Be Healthy!
Eat a healthy snack, for instance, popcorn!

 U.S. Government

Government Forms: Home and Abroad

The United States has a President who is elected by the people of the country as their leader. The United Kingdom has a Queen, or monarch. Italy is home to the Pope, who is the head of the Catholic Church but also has deep political ties to the government of the country. Types of government leadership can vary in countries from time to time for various reasons. Such changes may be mandated, forced or merely chosen by majority influence. The type of leaders, public offices and respective duties that are assigned to these government leaders are unique to the kind of government that exists in a land. Learning about the varieties of government systems is an interesting and often complicated matter. Confusion is possible when readers notice common vocabulary terms are used in very different styles of governments.

Directions: Use any resource you need to match each word with the definition.

_____ 1. All eligible citizens have an equal say in the decisions.	A. plutocracy
_____ 2. An older societal structure in which land is exchanged for work.	B. monarchy
_____ 3. Government rulers are elected or appointed rather than heir to the role.	C. oligarchy
_____ 4. Any form of government where one person is the supreme power.	D. totalitarianism
_____ 5. Government rule has no limits to its authority; it regulates everything.	E. republic
_____ 6. Power is controlled by a small number of people.	F. democracy
_____ 7. Characteristic of a government legislatively.	G. autocracy
_____ 8. One who represents another person legally.	H. theocracy
_____ 9. Official policy is governed by divine guidance.	I. constitutional
_____ 10. Government control by an oligarchy or the wealthy	J. representative
_____ 11. Government by a sovereignty in a single individual	K. feudalism

Creating an Outline

Once you have taken your notes, now it is time to organize your ideas. One way is to organize your ideas is by writing an outline, which arranges material in the order in which it is to be presented. Outlines have three basic parts: main ideas, subtopics, and supporting details. Main topics are listed with Roman numerals (I., II., III., etc.) and subtopics are indented and listed with capital letters (A., B., C.). Details that support those subtopics are indented further and listed with small letters. Rearrange the topics in the right column below into a formal outline in the left column. A few of the topics, subtopics and details, are filled in for you

First American Woman in Space

I. Early years of Sally Ride in California

    A. _____

    B. Educated at Westlake School for Girls

    C. _____

II. _____

    A. Applied to NASA as an astronaut

       1. Selected as NASA astronaut candidate

       2. _____

    B. _____

       1. First woman astronaut for NASA

       2. _____

    C. Other roles in U.S. space explorations

       1. _____

       2. _____

III. Pursuits in later life

    A. _____

    B. Partnered with Exxon to create STEM careers

Career in space sciences

Notable career highlights

Assigned to NASA headquarters in D.C.

Astronaut training at NASA

Started Sally Ride Science Company

Received B.S. degree in physics

Mission specialist assignments in flight

Born in Los Angeles, California

Honors and awards for contributions

DAY **4**

WEEK **8**

Strength

Be Healthy!
Smile!

DAILY EXERCISE
Chin-ups
"Stretch Before You Play!"

Instruction
Repeat 2 times

1+2=3
⊕ ⊖
⊗ ÷ =

Adding and Subtracting Integers

Rules: If both integers are positive or negative:
The sum of two positive integers is positive.
The sum of two negative integers is negative.
If one integer is positive and one is negative:
Subtract their absolute values and use
the sign of the greater absolute value.

Example:	- 3	+	- 5	= - 8
	9	+	11	= 20
	- 5	+	8	= 3
	8	-	5	= 3

Directions: Find each sum.

DAY 4

1. (-15) + 6 = _____

2. (-3) + 0 = _____

3. 6 + 21 = _____

4. (-5) + 12 = _____

5. (-4) + (-14) = _____

6. 7 + 13 = _____

7. (-30) + 29 = _____

8. (-17) + 6 = _____

9. (-5) + 20 = _____

10. 9 + (-23) = _____

11. 19 + 7 = _____

12. 0 - 27 = _____

13. (-18) - 11 = _____

14. (-27) - 11 = _____

15. 11 - (-30) = _____

16. 28 - (-23) = _____

17. 30 - 10 = _____

18. (-13) - 16 = _____

19. (-21) - 23 = _____

20. (-19) - (-16) = _____

21. (-21) - 26 = _____

WEEK 8

© Photo courtesy of the Terry Fox Foundation

Responsibility is the obligation to carry forward an assigned task to a successful conclusion even though it is quite difficult. When you are responsible, people can usually count on you.

Terrance Stanley Fox was a Canadian humanitarian, athlete and cancer research activist. In 1980, with one leg having been amputated, he embarked on a cross-Canada run to raise money and awareness for cancer research. Although the spread of cancer eventually forced him to end his quest after 143 days and 3,339 miles (5,373 kilometers), and ultimately cost him his life, his efforts resulted in a lasting, worldwide legacy. The annual Terry Fox Run, first held in 1981, has grown to involve millions of participants in over 60 countries and is now the world's largest one-day fundraiser for cancer research.

Fox was a distance runner and basketball player for his high school. His right leg was amputated in 1977 after he was diagnosed with cancer though he continued to run using an artificial leg. He also played wheelchair basketball in Vancouver, winning three national championships.

In 1980, he began the Marathon of Hope, a cross-country run to raise money for cancer research. Terry hoped to raise one dollar for each of Canada's 24 million people. He began with little fanfare from St. John's, Newfoundland, in April and ran the equivalent of a full marathon every day. Fox had become a national star by the time he reached Ontario. Fox was forced to end his run outside of Thunder Bay when the cancer spread to his lungs. His hopes of overcoming the disease and completing his marathon ended when he died nine months later.

Fox was the youngest person ever named Companion of the Order of Canada. He won the 1980 Lou Marsh Award as the nation's top sportsman and was named Canada's Newsmaker of the Year in both 1980 and 1981. Terry Fox is considered by many Canadians to be a national hero.

www.terryfox.org

Directions: Read each statement carefully. Then decide if the statement is True or False.

_____ 1. The annual Terry Fox Run, first held in 1980, has grown to involve millions.

_____ 2. Terry Fox began the Marathon of Hope, a cross-country run to raise money.

_____ 3. Fox had hoped to raise one dollar for each of Canada's 24 million people.

_____ 4. He was forced to end his run outside of St. John's, Newfoundland.

_____ 5. Terry was the youngest person ever named Companion of the Order of Canada.

☐ Organize a bake sale with friends or family to raise money for cancer research. Donate the money to an organization such as "Cookies For Kids' Cancer."

☐ Part of being responsible is admitting to your mistakes and accepting the consequences of your actions. Apologizing is one way to do this. Think of someone you have hurt with your words or actions. Apologize to them and ask for their forgiveness.

☐ Think about the saying, "When life gives you lemons, make lemonade." What does it mean? Write a passage on something difficult that you have gone through and how you reacted to the experience. Then ask yourself, were you responsible in your actions, and what did you do with the experiences.

Core Value Booklist
Read More About Responsibility

Responsibility
By Bruce Glassman

The Whipping Boy
By Sid Heischman

Diary of a Wimpy Kid
By Jeff Kinney

The Toothpaste Millionaire
By Jean Merrill

Shiloh Season
By Phyllis R. Naylor

Reading Extension
Activities at
SummerFitLearning.com

Let's Talk About It

Talk with your child about how to handle adversity and challenges in his/her life. Visit the website www.terryfox.org and learn more about Terry and how he chose to make a difference. Talk about how Terry Fox handled the challenge of losing his leg to cancer. Try to relate some of your own personal stories of hardship and how you took ownership in response to your own challenges.

1

2

3

DAY 5

WEEK 8

Play Time!

Choose a Game or Activity to Play for 60 minutes today!

YOU CHOOSE

_____

Write down which game or activity you played today!

Be Healthy!
Drink water instead of soda.

PARENT TIPS FOR WEEK 9

Skills of the Week

Weekly Value Perseverance

- ✔ Ordinal, Rational and Irrational numbers
- ✔ The Solar System
- ✔ Personal pronouns
- ✔ Choosing the Right Vocabulary Word
- ✔ History: The Cold War
- ✔ Fractions and Relations
- ✔ Statistics and probability
- ✔ Spelling Demons
- ✔ Writing an Argument
- ✔ Sequences of Events

Bethany Hamilton

Perseverance means not giving up or giving in when things are difficult. It means you try again when you fail.

Sometimes it is easy to forget that a lot of things in life require patience and hard work. Do not give up because it is hard to accomplish a task or to get something that we want. Focus on your goal and keep working hard. It is through this experience that you will accomplish what you want.

GET FIT TIME!

Play 60 Every Day!
Run, jump, dance and have fun outside every day for 60 minutes!

Weekly Extension Activities at SummerFitLearning.com

Perseverance In Action!
Color the star each day you show perseverance through your own actions.

Color the ☆ As You Complete Your Daily Task

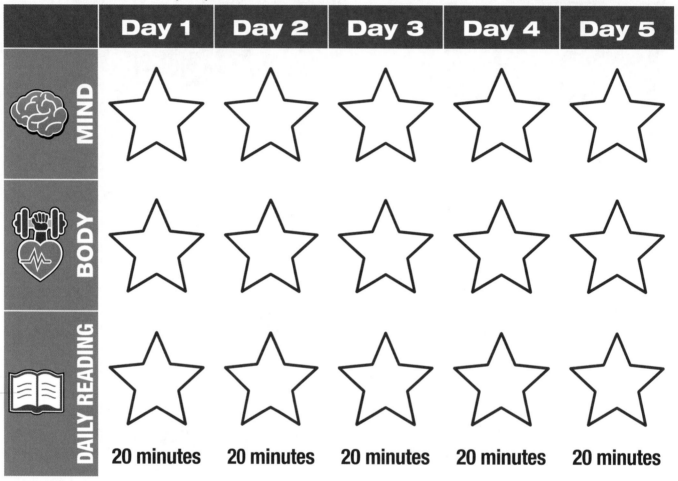

	Day 1	Day 2	Day 3	Day 4	Day 5
MIND	☆	☆	☆	☆	☆
BODY	☆	☆	☆	☆	☆
DAILY READING	☆ 20 minutes	☆ 20 minutes	☆ 20 minutes	☆ 20 minutes	☆ 20 minutes

You can do it!

"I have perseverance"

_____

Print Name

Ordinal, Rational, and Irrational Numbers

Directions: On a separate piece of paper prepare a number line so that zero is center most on the number line. Next, divide the segments on either side of zero proportionally to include: -4, -3, -2, -1, 1, 2, 3, 4. Properly record the numbers from the table on the number line. If the number is written in decimal or fraction form, do not change the number to an alternate form.

DAY 1

Rational Numbers	½	2.35	¾	2.0	1¾
Irrational Numbers	√3	√5	3.14159....	1.618...	√2

Directions: Compare: <, >, =

1. .50 _____ 3/5

2. 1/2 _____ 7/8

3. 4.87 _____ 4 3/8

4. 3/4 _____ .75

5. 1.35 _____ 22/11

6. 5/9 _____ .9

7. 1.54 _____ 54/6

8. .75 _____ 6/7

9. 7/8 _____ .78

10. .85 _____ .52

11. 1/2 _____ .34

12. 1.67 _____ 1 6/7

Multimedia Activity: Use an online calculator to test fractional numbers through division to see if a terminating or repeated decimal is found. Pi or 3.14159 . . . is a famous irrational number. Look online for other notable irrational numbers.

Aerobic
Go to www.summerfitlearning.com for more Activities!

DAILY EXERCISE	Instruction	Be Healthy!
Hide-and-Seek	**Get your family and**	Brush your teeth in the morning, afternoon and before bed
"Stretch Before You Play!"	**friends to play**	

 **Astronomy**

The Solar System

The more appropriate and current model of the solar system is heliocentric. Planetary movement around the Sun happens in somewhat circular orbits. Planets differ in size, composition, distance from the Sun and, therefore, gravitational differences, too. The Sun occupies the majority of the system's mass and those objects orbiting the sun lie within a flat disc-like area called the ecliptic plane. Mostly composed of rock and metal, Mercury, Venus, Earth and Mars are called the terrestrial planets. The other four, known as gas giants, are known to be much larger and are made mostly of hydrogen and helium. The two largest are Jupiter and Saturn. Neptune and Uranus consist mostly of ices such as water, ammonia and methane and are commonly called "ice giants." Among the planets are much smaller, less significant system masses such as comets and asteroids. Moons also accompany many planets following gravitational, orbital paths. The asteroid belt, which lies between Mars and Jupiter, is similar to the terrestrial planets as it is composed mainly of rock and metal. Kepler's laws of planetary motion describes the orbits of objects about the Sun, and prove that objects closer to the Sun travel more quickly because they are more affected by the Sun's gravity.

Directions: Create a modern, heliocentric solar system diagram below. Include the main 12 solar system features noted in the paragraph.

A **subjective pronoun** acts as the subject of a sentence—it performs the action of the predicate. Subjective pronouns are *he, I, it, she, they, we,* and *you*. Example: **He** opened the door quickly.

An **objective pronoun** acts as the object of a sentence—it receives the action of the predicate. The objective pronouns are *her, him, it, me, them, us,* and *you*. Example: Al called her on his cell.

Directions: Underline the correct personal pronoun. Write **S** for subjective and **O** for objective.

_____ 1. Chuck and (me, I) arrived late for the swimming class.

_____ 2. Just between you and (I, me), I have always hated writing poem.

_____ 3. Olivia said that she recognized (he, him) immediately.

_____ 4. Our neighbors drove (we, us) girls to the train station.

_____ 5. No one knows where (she, her) and I have been.

_____ 6. Mother was glad that (they, them) were coming to the birthday party.

_____ 7. Please show Sarah and (she, her) your pictures of the wedding.

_____ 8. The search party safely found Dwayne and (he, him) in the woods.

Choosing the Correct Vocabulary Word

Directions: Write the letter from Column B that is appropriate for the numbered word in Column A.

Column A	Column B
_____ 9. detain	a. not the same; different
_____ 10. custody	b. showing too much pride in oneself
_____ 11. arrogant	c. more than enough; plentiful
_____ 12. violate	d. full of feverish activity, haste, or confusion
_____ 13. arid	e. to keep from going on; to stop
_____ 14. sanctuary	f. having a little or no rainfall; very dry
_____ 15. hectic	g. magnificent; very impressive
_____ 16. splendor	h. control over; supervision or care
_____ 17. distinct	i. to break, as a law or a promise
_____ 18. abundant	j. a place of safety or a shelter

Strength

Go to www.summerfitlearning.com for more Activities!

DAILY EXERCISE
Crunches
"Stretch Before You Play!"

Instruction
Repeat 5 times

Be Healthy!
Turn off the TV and play outside.

History

The Cold War was a twentieth century conflict between the United States of America, the Soviet Union and their respective allies, over political, economic and military issues, often described as a struggle between capitalism and communism. In Europe, this meant the U.S. led West and NATO on one side and Soviet led East and the Warsaw Pact on the other. It lasted from 1945 to the collapse of the USSR in 1991.

Word Bank

Chernobyl
Cuba
Cuban Exiles
Iron Curtain
Kremlin
Khrushchev
NATO
Thaw
Truman
Warsaw Pact

Across

5. alliance of US, Canada and countries of Western Europe
6. US president who resisted Communism during the Cold War
8. ruler of Soviet Union during the Thaw
9. time when citizens of Soviet Union began to have greater freedoms
10. site of a nuclear energy plant disaster

Down

1. placement of missiles caused a crisis during 1962
2. invisible wall that separated the Warsaw Pact countries from Western Europe.
3. An alliance of Eastern European countries behind the Iron Curtain
4. Bay of Pigs invaders
7. the site of the Soviet Union Government

DAY 2 · 4 · 5 · WEEK 9

Directions: Apply the function rules given to solve for the y values. List answers as ordered pairs.

1.

x value:	Function Rule: multiply by 2, then add 1	y value:	Ordered Pair:
1	2( ) + 1		
2	2( ) + 1		
3	2( ) + 1		
4	2( ) + 1		
5	2( ) + 1		

2.

x value:	Function Rule: multiply by 5, then add 1	y value:	Ordered Pair:
1	5( ) + 1		
2	5( ) + 1		
3	5( ) + 1		
4	5( ) + 1		
5	5( ) + 1		

3.

x value:	Function Rule: multiply by -2, then add 3	y value:	Ordered Pair:
1	-2( ) + 3		
2	-2( ) + 3		
3	-2( ) + 3		
4	-2( ) + 3		
5	-2( ) + 3		

4.

x value:	Function Rule: multiply by 3, then add -1	y value:	Ordered Pair:
1	3( ) + (-1)		
2	3( ) + (-1)		
3	3( ) + (-1)		
4	3( ) + (-1)		
5	3( ) + (-1)		

Be Healthy!
Slow down when you eat!

DAILY EXERCISE
Hula-Hoop
"Stretch Before You Play!"

Instruction
Goal = 20 times without dropping

Statistics and Probability

Independent Events in Probability

Events are **independent** when the outcome of an event does not influence the outcome of the second.

Example: In the following independent events, if two pennies are flipped, what is the probability that two heads will be flipped? Use a tree diagram to find the probability.

Let H = Heads and T = Tails; "P" stands for "probability".

P (two heads) = number of times two heads occur

Total number of outcomes = 1/4	The probability that you flip two heads is 1/4.

Directions: Find the probability for each of the following:

1. A bag has 4 green beads and 6 purple beads. What is the probability of picking a green bead?

2. A vase has 28 flowers. There are 17 yellow flowers and 11 pink ones. What is the probability of picking a yellow one?

Spelling Demons

Directions: Underline the correctly spelled word in the following phrases.

1. a (brief, breif) lecture

2. (weather, whether) or not to study

3. found on the (cieling, ceiling)

4. chocolate cake for (desert, dessert)

5. driving (passed, past) the theater

6. very (course, coarse) cloth

7. (neither, niether) one of those books

8. three (copies, copys) of that document

9. some good (advice, advise) on that topic

10. many (heros, heroes) in that movie

11. (chief, cheif) of the police department

12. gave an (apoligy, apology) to Rose

13. was (conscious, consceous) when found

14. very (leisurely, liesurely) vacation this year

15. considered a very (peculair, peculiar) lady

16. a (necessery, necessary) move this month

17. (grabbed, grabed) the purse and ran

18. (indiciate, indicate) the problem to complete

19. expressed (loneliness, lonliness) all week

20. during these (econmic, economic) times

Ambiguous Reference

Ambiguous reference occurs when a pronoun refers confusingly to two antecedents so that the reader does not know at once which antecedent (the word to which a pronoun refers) is meant.

Directions: Write who or what the underlined pronoun may refer to.

Example: Jason noticed that the actor was smiling in a odd way as <u>he</u> came down the aisle. (In this sentence, he can refer to either Jason or the actor.)

21. Mrs. Carlson gave the Red Cross all her money, and this is the reason why <u>she</u> declared bankruptcy.

_____

22. The boat bumped the edge of the dock, but <u>it</u> did not need many repairs.

_____

23. Katy's sister wondered if <u>she</u> were tall enough to be a model.

_____

DAILY EXERCISE
Squats
"Stretch Before You Play!"

Instruction
Repeat 6 Times

Be Healthy!
Walk with your family before or after dinner.

1
2

Writing

Writing an Argument

What is an argument? An argument is a form of writing that tries to convince readers to believe or to do something. An argument, which includes facts and examples, has a strong point of view about a problem or an idea. Your assignment is to introduce claim(s) and organize your reasons and evidence. Use words, phrases, and clauses to clarify the relationships among your claim(s) and reasons. Finally, provide a concluding statement that follows your argument.

DAY
4

WEEK 9

_____

_____

_____

_____

_____

_____

_____

_____

_____

There are a lot of words that can be used to describe the meaning of perseverance, but the most commonly used word is commitment.

Spoungeworthy Photo by Phil Stefans

On October 31, 2003, Bethany Hamilton went for a morning surf along Tunnels Beach, Kauai. About 7:30 AM, she was lying on her surfboard with her left arm dangling in the water, when a 14-15 foot long tiger shark attacked her, ripping her left arm off just below the shoulder. Despite the trauma of the incident, Bethany was determined to return to surfing and did get back into the water. Less than a month after the incident, she returned to her board and went surfing again. Initially, Bethany adopted a custom-made board that was longer and slightly thicker, making it easier to paddle. After teaching herself to surf with one arm, on January 10, 2004, Hamilton entered a major competition.

In July 2004, she won the Best Comeback Athlete ESPY Award. In addition, she was presented with a special "courage award" at the 2004 Teen Choice Awards for her true perseverance. In 2005, Bethany took 1st place in the National Scholastic Surfing Association (NSSA) National Championships, a goal she had been trying to achieve since before the shark attack. In her first competition against many of the world's best women surfers, she finished 2nd. In 2004, MTV Books published Hamilton's book, Soul Surfer: A True Story of Faith, Family, and Fighting to Get Back on the Board, which describes her ordeal. Her story is also told in the 2007 short subject documentary film, Heart of a Soul Surfer, which addresses her courage and determination. Then, in 2008, she began competing full time on the Association of Surfing Professionals World (ASP) World Qualifying Series.

Directions: Sequence by numbering the following events from the oldest to the most recent.

_____ She began competing full time in 2008 on the Association of Surfing Professional World.

_____ In July 2004 Bethany won the Best Comeback Athlete ESPY Award.

_____ Bethany was attacked by a 14-15 foot long tiger shark, ripping off her left arm.

_____ In 2007 *Heart of a Soul Surfer* was made into a documentary film.

_____ In 2005, Bethany took 1st place in the National Scholastic Surfing Association.

_____ Less than a month after the incident, she returned to her board and went surfing again.

_____ In 2004, MTV Books published *Soul Surfer: A True Story of Faith, Family and Fighting*.

_____ In her first competition against the world's best women surfers, she finished 2nd.

_____ Hamilton was presented a special "courage award" at the 2004 Teen Choice Awards.

_____ She adopted a custom-made board that was longer and slightly thicker.

☐ Make a large star and decorate it. Write the words "Reach for the stars" on one side. On the other side write something you would like to accomplish. Think about the ways you can accomplish your goal.

Core Value Booklist
Read More About Perseverance

I Know Why the Caged Bird Sings
By Maya Angelou

Three Cups of Tea
By Greg Mortenson

Holes
By Louis Sachar

Oh, The Places You'll Go
By Dr. Seuss

Hatchet
By Gary Paulsen

Reading Extension Activities at SummerFitLearning.com

☐ Compose a rap or song about perseverance and share it with your family or friends.

☐ Study the life of Helen Keller. What obstacles did she have to overcome to persevere as a deaf and blind person? Blindfold yourself and see what challenges come with being blind.

☐ Make a bookmark with the saying "Never, never, never give up" by Winston Churchill.

Let's Talk About It

Even though it is hard, resist jumping in when you see your child struggling with something. If you always step in to help, it can lead to a cycle of dependency. Rather, talk with your child and let him/her know you believe in them. Reinforce in them their abilities, and you will give them the esteem and confidence they need to complete their project.

1
2
3

DAY 5

WEEK 9

Play Time!

Choose a Game or Activity to Play for 60 minutes today!

YOU CHOOSE

_____
Write down which game or activity you played today!

Be Healthy!
Do something active everyday.

PARENT TIPS FOR WEEK 10

Skills of the Week

✔ Improving Language Usage
✔ Geometry - Surface Area
✔ European Geography Scramble
✔ Physical Changes
✔ Reading Comprehension
✔ Writing a Narrative
✔ Conservation and Pollution
✔ Recognizing Standard English

Weekly Value Friendship

Lewis and Clark

Friendship is what comes from being friends. It is caring and sharing and being there for each other in good times and bad.

It is fun to have friends that we play with, go to the movies and share our time, but it also is a responsibility. Our friends are people that we trust, protect, respect and stand up for even when it is not easy. We care about our friends and our friends care about us.

GET FIT TIME!

Play 60 Every Day!
Run, jump, dance and have fun outside every day for 60 minutes!

Weekly Extension Activities at SummerFitLearning.com

Friendship In Action!
Color the star each day you show friendship through your own actions.

WEEK 10
HEALTHY MIND + HEALTHY BODY

Color the ⭐ As You Complete Your Daily Task

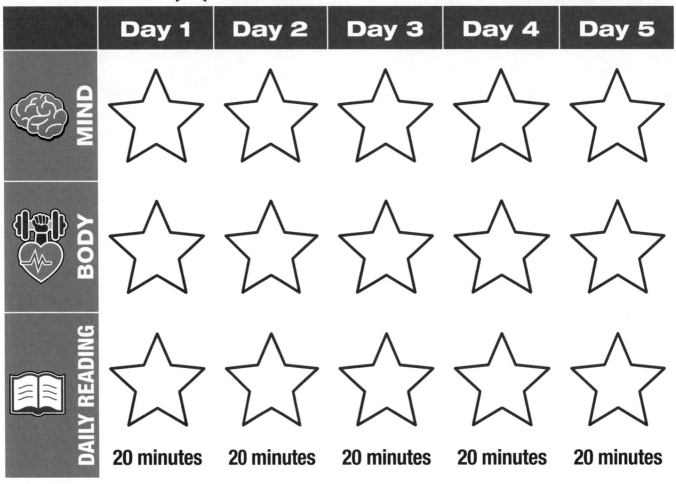

	Day 1	Day 2	Day 3	Day 4	Day 5
MIND	☆	☆	☆	☆	☆
BODY	☆	☆	☆	☆	☆
DAILY READING	☆	☆	☆	☆	☆
	20 minutes	20 minutes	20 minutes	20 minutes	20 minutes

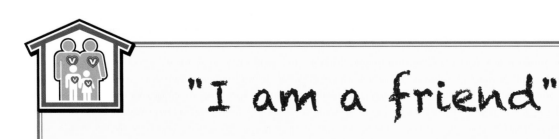

You can do it!

"I am a friend"

_____
Print Name

Directions: Read the following paragraphs. Select the numbered sentence that does not belong.

1. The night was filled with unbelievable excitement. 2. Everyone was there, hiding somewhere in the house, waiting in anticipation. 3. The family had planned this surprise for weeks. 4. Billy's uncle had been to Europe for the third time. 5. Billy was coming home from the hospital and today was his birthday. 6. What a great night this is going to be for our family.

   A. Sentence 1   B. Sentence 2   C. Sentence 4   D. Sentence 5

2. The wind is blowing gently across the lawn and a squirrel is scampering about the lawn. 2. Fall is in the air, and some of the leaves are already changing their colors. 3. I cannot do these math problems my teacher assigned for the weekend. 4. Several birds are dipping down now and then for a quick worm or a drink of water from the fountain. 5. Another change of seasons is upon us, and I am so lucky to be a part of it.

   A. Sentence 1   B. Sentence 2   C. Sentence 4   D. Sentence 5

Directions: Read the following sentences and choose the sentence which is the best combination of the ideas presented.

3. Darriel went on a Canadian tour with me. Darriel is a high school student.

   A. Darriel went on a Canadian tour with me and now is a high school student.

   B. Darriel, a high school student, went on a Canadian tour with me.

   C. Darriel is a high school student, and he went on a Canadian tour with me.

   D. Even though Darriel is a high school student, he went on a Canadian tour with me.

4. Felipe is a foreign exchange student. Felipe is from Lima, Peru. Felipe attends Lakeside High School.

   A. Felipe is a foreign exchange student from Lima, Peru, and he attends Lakeside High School.

   B. Felipe, a foreign exchange student, is from Lima, Peru, and Felipe attends Lakeside High School.

   C. Felipe, a foreign exchange student from Lima, Peru, attends Lakeside High School.

   D. Felipe is a foreign exchange student and is from Lima, Peru, and attends Lakeside High School.

DAY 1

DAILY EXERCISE
Jogging for Fitness 15
"Stretch Before You Play!"

Instruction
Jog 15 minutes in place or outside

Be Healthy!
Eat more whole grains like pasta, bread and rice.

Geometry - Surface Area

Finding the surface area of a solid figure is a series of calculations of the faces of the figure. It is necessary to find the surface area when attempting to cover a figure's outer faces.

The box below has commonly sought surface area formulas and figures.

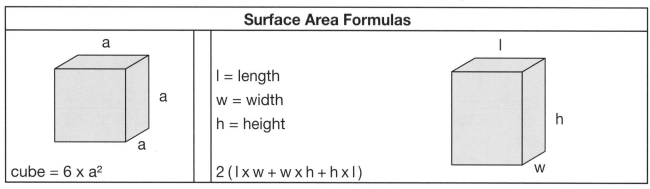

Surface Area Formulas

l = length
w = width
h = height

cube = 6 x a²

2 (l x w + w x h + h x l)

Directions: Find the surface area for the following figures.

1. A = _____cm²

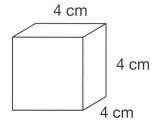

4 cm
4 cm
4 cm

2. A = _____ cm²

12 cm
6 cm
6 cm
6 cm

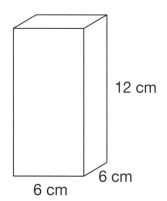

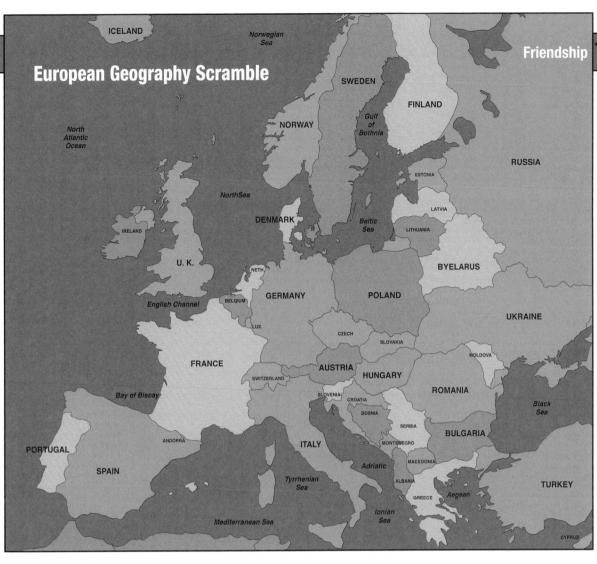

European Geography Scramble

Friendship

Directions: Unscramble the letters below to form names of some of the European countries. Then locate each country.

_____ 1. A I R T S U A

_____ 2. L O P T A G U R

_____ 3. R E C E G E

_____ 4. A N D P O L

_____ 5. N E D E W S

_____ 6. A G A B U I R L

_____ 7. L F D N I A N

_____ 8. G E M B L U I

_____ 9. N A M K D R E

_____ 10. L A T Y I

_____ 11. N R E A F C

_____ 12. R A N Y W O

_____ 13. M E N G R Y A

_____ 14. A N S I P

_____ 15. C L D I E N A

_____ 16. A I N A M O R

DAILY EXERCISE
Lunges
"Stretch Before You Play!"

Instruction
Repeat 5 times
with each leg

Be Healthy!
Learn a new joke today and tell it at dinner.

DAY 2

4

5

WEEK 10

Physical Changes

The earth is affected by changes to its surface through weathering. Weathering is the process that breaks down rock and other substances. Damage to soil affects the preservation of fossils, and fossils provide scientists with important information about the history of our earth. Fossil preservation relates to what organic material is deposited and where. They lend insight to interpreting past environmental conditions, plate movement and previous life forms. Through intensive farming and reducing forest covers, humans have changed the earth's surface.

Moving of particles through water and wind is known as **erosion**. This wearing away of material on the surface of earth creates deposits of sediments. These sediments, over time, collect or pile up. Weathered or eroded rock sediment is the basic "ingredient" of soil. Soil characteristics, such as texture, fertility, and ability to withstand erosion, are determined by the decomposed [organic] material it contains.

Human activities, such as reducing forest cover and intensive farming, have changed the earth's surface over many years. Humans have the ability to have a positive or negative impact on the surface of the earth. Some human activities can actually accelerate erosion. It is important to conserve our natural resources of water, soil and air. Much of erosion is natural and unchangeable by humans. However, being irresponsible with our natural resources will have a negative impact on the surface of our Earth. Harmful or thoughtless human actions can actually cause erosion to accelerate.

Directions: Answer the following questions with accurate, thorough answers, in your own words.

1. Describe erosion and its effects on earth._____

_____

2. Explain the difference between weathering and deposition. _____

_____

3. Describe ways humans accelerate erosion and how this adversely affects the earth's

   resources. _____

_____

4. Explain what benefit fossils provide humans. _____

_____

The Brain: A Message Center

The brain is the largest and most important part of a person's nervous system. The human brain is approximately 3 1/2 pounds of gray and white gelatin-like substance. The brain weighs only one-fiftieth as much as the body, yet it uses one-fourth of the blood's oxygen. The biggest part of the brain is the cerebrum, which makes up 85% of the brain's weight. The cerebrum is the thinking part of the brain. It knows how to put facts and ideas together as well as how to figure out problems. The brain is an information storage space and a how-to library. So you cannot dance or kick a soccer ball without your cerebrum.

The brain is also a drugstore that fills its own prescriptions in split seconds. When you are hurt, for example, the brain sends out a chemical called "enkephalin," which is a pain-killer. When you encounter a potential danger, the brain sends a chemical called "norepinephrine" through your body which in turn starts another chemical called "adrenaline" flowing to warn you of danger.

The brain is a message center, too. It is like a big telephone exchange with messages coming in and out all the time. Each second the brain receives more than 100 million nerve messages from your body, and it knows what to do with them.

Directions: After reading the passage above, answer the questions with the best answer.

1. The largest part of the brain is the
   A. enkephalin.   B. cerebrum.   C. adrenaline.   D. norepinephrine.

2. Which of the following substances warns the body about danger?
   A. adrenaline   B. prescription   C. enkephalin   D. norepinephrine

3. A simile is a comparison that uses like or as. Which of the following is used in a simile that compares the brain to something else?
   A. gelatin-like substance   B. nervous system
   C. telephone exchange   D. information storage system

4. A metaphor is a comparison that does not use like or as. Which of the following is not a metaphor for the brain?
   A. how-to library   B. message center   C. drugstore   D. gray and white substance

5. The author of this selection uses the fact that the brain uses one-fourth of the blood's oxygen to show
   A. how small the brain is.   B. that the brain knows how to put facts and ideas together.
   C. how important the brain is.   D. that the brain is good storage space.

Aerobic

Go to www.summerfitlearning.com for more Activities!

Go to www.summerfitlearning.com for more Activities!

DAILY EXERCISE
Jump Rope
"Stretch Before You Play!"

Instruction
Goal = 3 minutes
without stopping

Be Healthy!
Turn off the TV
when you eat.

Writing a Narrative

Writing a Narrative

Narrative writing is writing that tells a story, whether true or fictional. A narrative follows a sequence of events and, therefore, must have a beginning, middle, and an end. Engage your reader by establishing a narrator and/or characters. Organize an event sequence that unfolds naturally. Then, use narrative techniques, such as dialogue, pacing, and description, to develop experiences, events and/or characters. Finally, provide a conclusion that follows from the narrated experiences and events. Use the space below to organize your thoughts; then type your narrative on your computer.

DAY 3

WEEK 10

Conservation & Pollution

Conservation is a way to break old patterns that have harmed the earth and threatened our natural resources. It is imperative for humans to control pollution and begin working hard to be well aware of ways to protect our natural resources and thus, conserve. Conserve means to use less, or reduce or make adjustments so that there is less waste. It is possible to do this by taking certain measures in our daily lives. Below is a chart listing ways to conserve and protect natural resources. There are some empty boxes on the chart for other ways conservation can be implemented. Based on what information is given, add to the list other ways of conservation.

ACTIVITY:	NATURAL RESOURCE CONSERVED	FREQUENCY
farming	soil, water	annually
water a lawn	water	daily/weekly
monitor vehicle emissions	air	annually
no dumping in lakes	water	daily
composting	soil	weekly/monthly

Multimedia Link:

Work with your family or a friend and begin researching on the Internet various environmental protection groups that advocate conservation. Consider what tips are given, how possible they are to put into practice and write an email to someone to find out more ways you can help or begin to be a voice for earth conservation. Use the space below to record those friends, relatives or neighbors whom you have contacted.

Strength
Go to www.summerfitlearning.com for more Activities!

DAILY EXERCISE
Bottle Lift
"Stretch Before You Play!"

Instruction
Repeat 10 times

Be Healthy!
Plan a meal for your family.

Recognizing Standard English

The exercises have been carefully selected with emphasis on language usage and expression. Write the letter in the blank that best completes each sentence.

_____ 1. Amia had been _____ a beautiful necklace for her birthday.
   A. gave   B. given   C. give   D. gaven

_____ 2. Zackary was very late so he ran _____ to catch the bus.
   A. quick   B. quicker   C. quickly   D. quickest

_____ 3. _____ were the winners of the swimming relay competition in the Olympics.
   A. Their   B. Them   C. Us   D. They

_____ 4. During the heavy rain the ripest tomatoes had _____ open.
   A. burst   B. bursted   C. bust   D. busted

_____ 5. When we were flying to Tampa, strong winds _____ us off our course.
   A. blow   B. blew   C. blowed   D. blown

_____ 6. _____ both going to Oak Ridge Summer Camp next year.
   A. They   B. They're   C. They've   D. They'll

_____ 7. We had _____ for miles in the dense fog.
   A. driven   B. drove   C. drived   D. drive

_____ 8. Using the Internet is the _____ way to acquire information.
   A. quickly   B. quickest   C. more quick   D. most quickest

_____ 9. Marcia and I _____ planning to run in the park early tomorrow morning.
   A. wasn't   B. is   C. are   D. was

____10. Aunt Emily had never _____ on an airplane before.
   A. flied   B. flew   C. flying   D. flown

____11. Although I had worked very hard, he _____ more orange juice than I did.
   A. drank   B. had drank   C. drunk   D. had drunk

____12. Charlie had _____ his mother a letter from summer camp.
   A. wrote   B. written   C. write   D. wroten

____13. When the news was announced, I _____ to regret my choice.
   A. begin   B. begun   C. began   D. begann

____14. You can pass to the seventh grade _____ you complete the sixth grade.
   A. during   B. before   C. after   D. meantime

____15. It has been a long time since I have _____ from you.
   A. here   B. hear   C. he're   D. heard

DAY 4

WEEK 10

Friendship is a relationship between two people who hold mutual affection for each other. The value of friendship is often the result of friends consistently demonstrating mutual understanding and compassion.

The **Lewis and Clark Expedition**, also known as the Corps of Discovery Expedition (1804-1806), was the first transcontinental expedition to the Pacific coast undertaken by the United States. This expedition was commissioned by President Thomas Jefferson and led by two Virginia veterans of Indian wars in the Ohio Valley, Meriwether Lewis and William Clark. Lewis and Clark were friends over 200 years ago when the U.S. was still a new country. According to President Jefferson, they were to explore the Missouri River and to discover and chart a passage to the Pacific Ocean. Along the way, Jefferson wanted Lewis and Clark to begin trading with the Native American tribes, discover new plants and animals, and make maps and charts of their course so that others could follow.

Their voyage, which would become the most famous journey of exploration in American history, would last more than two years and take them in excess of 2,700 miles beyond the United States' existing borders. The two friends faced unknown dangers, obstacles, and hardships as they forged their way from the Mississippi River west to the Pacific Ocean.

In its course, the Corps of Discovery would explore breathtaking landscape inhabited by a host of proud Indian nations and an overwhelming abundance of wildlife--the northern American West before it was changed forever by white settlements. Their experiences, chronicled in the journals, constitute an authentic American epic. Through all of their perils, Lewis and Clark stood by each other and showed extraordinary teamwork, bravery, and loyalty.

Directions: Fill in the blanks using words from the passage.

1. Lewis and Clark's expedition lasted more than _____ years, from _____ to _____.

2. President _____ commissioned the first transcontinental expedition.

3. The expedition would take Lewis and Clark from the _____ River

to the _____ Ocean.

4. The Lewis and Clark Expedition was also known as the _____.

5. Name at least three reasons for this expedition: _____

_____

_____

Choose 1 or more activities to do with your family or friends. Color today's star when you are finished. Good job!

☐ Write an essay about friendship. Write about what being a friend means to you. What do true friends do? What shouldn't they do? How do friends behave and what happens when friends argue or disagree?

☐ Make a card to invite a friend over. When they arrive, let them choose the activity you will do.

☐ Make some cookies for a new kid in the neighborhood, or go over and introduce yourself. Introduce the new kid to the rest of the kids in the neighborhood.

Core Value Booklist
Read More About Friendship

Number the Stars
By Lois Lowry

A Bridge to Terabithia
By Katherine Paterson

Shoeshine Girl
By Robert Bulla

Jenny Wren
By Dawn Watkins

Shiloh
By Phyllis R. Naylor

Reading Extension Activities at SummerFitLearning.com

Let's Talk About It

Discuss with your child the difference between having a good friend who they really know and having a lot that they don't really know. In today's world, social networks and web sites can add to the confusion about what friendship really means and the importance of having a few real friends.

Play Time!

Choose a Game or Activity to Play for 60 minutes today!

YOU CHOOSE

Write down which game or activity you played today!

Be Healthy!
Tell someone "I love you."

Sidebar: 1 2 3 DAY 5 WEEK 10

EXTRAS
Fitness Index
Family Health and Wellness Tips
Summer Journal • Book Report
Answer Key • Certificate of Completion

FITNESS INDEX

A healthy life is an active life. Kids need to be physically active for 60 minutes a day. Use the daily fitness activity to get moving. After 10 weeks of physical activity you have created a new and healthy lifestyle!

AEROBIC

Aerobic Exercise = Oxygen

The word "Aerobic" means "needing or giving oxygen." These *Summer Fit* exercises get the heart pumping and oxygen moving to help burn off sugars and calories!

STRENGTH

Strength Exercise = Muscle

Strength exercises help make muscles stronger. These *Summer Fit* exercises help build strong muscles to support doing fun activities around the house, school and outdoors!

SPORTS

Play Exercise = Sport Activity

Playing a different sport each week is an opportunity to use the *Summer Fit* oxygen and fitness exercises in a variety of ways. There are a lot of sports to choose from and remember that the most important thing about being *Summer Fit* is to have fun and play!

Warm Up Before Exercising

1 **Inchworm** – Put your hand on the ground in front of your feet. Walked out on the hands and then walk up on the feet. Do this 5 times.

2 **Knee Hug** – While you are slowly walking, pull your knee to your chest and hug. Do this 5 times on each leg.

3 **Toe Grab** – Toe Touch. Grab the toe behind your leg then touch the opposite toe with your opposite hand. Stand up and switch. Repeat 5 tines on each leg.

Warning:

Before starting any new exercise program you should consult your family physician. Even children can have medical conditions and at risk conditions that could limit the amount of physical activity they can do. So check with your doctor and then

Get Fit!

Aerobic Exercise = Oxygen

Aerobic exercises get you moving. When you move your heart pumps faster and more oxygen gets to your lungs. Movement helps burn off sugars and calories and gets you fit!

◆ **Jogging for Fitness 5**: Jog 5 minutes in place or outside:

◆ **Jogging for Fitness 10**: Jog 10 minutes in place or outside:

◆ **Jogging for Fitness 15**: Jog 15 minutes in place our outside:

◆ **Jumping Jacks:** Jump to a position with your legs spread wide and your hands touching overhead and then returning to a position with your feet together and arms at your sides. A more intense version is to bend down (over) and touch the floor in between each jump. **Goal = 20 Jumping Jacks**

◆ **Let's Jump:** Jump forward and back, jump side to side. Hop on one foot to another, moving side-to-side, alternating feet. Quicken your pace. Repeat. **Goal = 3 Sets of Jumps**

◆ **Let's Dance:** Step to your right with your right foot (putting your weight on your right foot). Step behind your right foot with your left foot (putting your weight on your left foot). Step again to the right with your right foot (weight on right) and touch your left foot next to your right (with your weight staying on the right foot). Repeat the above going left but switching to the other foot. **Goal = Dance for 5 minutes**

Do the Cha-cha
Step forward right, cha-cha
Step forward left, cha-cha
Repeat

Do the Cross over
Cross right over left, kick out right leg then backwards
cha-cha-cha
Cross left over right, kick out left leg then backwards
cha-cha-cha
Repeat

Do the Rope
Rope 1/4 to the left
1/4 facing the rear
1/4 turn left again
Rope to the front and step together with a clap.
Repeat
(When you "rope" hold one hand above your head and swing your arms in a circle like you have a rope above you).

> **Watch exercise training videos at:**
> **SummerFitLearning.com**

◆ **Pass and Go/Get a Friend to Play this Game With You!:** This activity requires a second person. Ask a friend or someone from your family to play with you. The object of this activity is to pass a ball back and forth counting by 2's get to a 100 as fast as you can. Have a stopwatch handy. Set a time you want to beat and go! Increase your goal by setting a lower time. Repeat. **Goal = 100**

◆ **Step It Up/ Start Slow & Increase Your Speed:** This activity uses stairs if you have them. If you do, take three trips up and down the stairs. Raise your legs high like you are in a marching band. If you do not have stairs, do 20 step-ups on one step. **Goal = 20 steps**

- **Kangaroo Bounce:** Tape a shoelace to the floor in a straight line. Stand on one side of the string with both feet together. Jump forward over the string and then backward to land in your original place. Take a short break—and do it again. This time jump side-to-side over the shoelace. **Goal = 10 Times**

- **Hoops - Play to 11 by 1's:** A trash can makes a great indoor basketball goal— perfect for a quick game of one-on-one against yourself or a friend! Use a bottle-cap or crunched up ball of paper as your basketball. Twist, jump and make sure to use a few fakes to win the game! **Goal = 11**

- **Green Giant:** Mow the grass, weed the garden or pick up the yard.

- **Capture the Flag/ Get Your Family and Friends to Play:** Use scarves or old T-shirts for flags. Use a different color one for each team. Use chalk, cones, tape, or landmarks such as trees or sidewalks to divide your playing area into equal-sized territories for each team. Place one flag into each territory. It must be visible and once it is placed it cannot be moved. When the game begins, players cross into opposing teams' territories to grab their flags. When a player is in an opposing team's territory he/she can be captured by that team's players. If they tag him/her, he/she must run to the sideline and perform an exercise—for example, five jumping jacks or three push-ups. After they perform their exercise the player can go back to his/her own team's territory and resume play. The game ends when one team successfully captures the flag(s) from the other team or teams and returns to their own territory with the opposing team's flag.

- **Happy Feet:** Use your feet every chance you get today. Walk to a friend's house, to the store, around the park or wherever it's safe to walk. **Goal = Get your parents to walk with you after dinner**

- **Let's Roll:** Put your lungs to work on your bike, skates or scooter. Don't forget to wear helmets and pads!

- **Speed:** Rest in between. See how fast you and your friends can run for one block. Time yourself and see if you can beat your original time. Repeat. **Goal = 2 blocks**

- **Hopscotch:** Toss a stone into the first square. The stone must land completely within the designated square without touching a line or bouncing out. Hop through the course, skipping the square with the marker in it. Single squares must be hopped on one foot. After hopping into "home" turn around and return through the course until you reach the square with their marker. Retrieve the marker and continue the course as stated without touching a line or stepping into a square with another player's marker. Upon successfully completing the sequence, toss the marker into square number two, and repeat the pattern. You cannot step on a line, miss a square, or lose balance. Complete one course for every numbered square.

- **Tag/ Get your family and friends to play:** A group of players (two or more) decide who is going to be "it", often using a counting-out game such as eeny, meeny, miny, moe. The player selected to be "it" chases the others, attempting to get close enough to tag them—touching them with a hand—while the others try to escape. A tag makes the tagged player "it" - in some variations, the previous "it" is no longer "it" and the game can continue indefinitely, while in others, both players remain "it" and the game ends when all players have become "it."

- **Hide-and-Seek/ Get your family and friends to play:** This is a game in which a number of players conceal themselves in the environment, to be found by one or more seekers. The game is played by one player (designated as being "it") counting to a predetermined number while the other players hide. After reaching the number, the player who is "it" tries to find the other players.
  After the player designated as "it" finds another player, the found player must run to base, before s/he is tagged by "it." After the first player is caught they help the "it" seek out others. Last one found wins!

- **Hula-Hoop:** A hula-hoop is a toy hoop that is twirled around your waist, limbs or neck. Use your hips to twirl the hoop around your body as many times as you can. Set a time goal and work to reach it without letting the hoop drop to the ground. As you get better extend your goal! **Goal = 20 times without dropping**

- **Jump Rope:** is the primary tool used in the game of skipping where you jump over a rope swung so that it passes under your feet and over your head. Here are some different jumps that you can do:
  Basic jump or easy jump: This is where both feet are slightly apart and jump at the same time over the rope. Beginners should master this technique first before moving onto more advanced techniques.
  Alternate foot jump (speed step): This style consists of using alternate feet to jump off the ground. This technique can be used to effectively double the number of skips per minute as compared to the above technique. This step is used for speed events.
  Criss-Cross: This method is similar to the basic jump with the only difference being that while jumping, the left hand goes to the right part of the body and vice versa for the right hand, with arms crossing in front of the body.
  Side Swing: This is a basic technique where the rope passes the side of the skipper's body, without jumping it. Usually the skipper performs a basic jump after a side swing, or a criss-cross.

Strength Exercise = Muscle

Strength exercises make muscles stronger. When you build strong muscles you are able to lift more, run faster, and do fun activities around your house, school, and outdoors!

◆ **Knee lifts:** Stand with your feet flat on the floor. Start by lifting your right knee up 5 times, always bring both feet together between each interval then change legs. When you feel more confident, bounce while you bring your knee up and alternate between legs. **Goal = repeat 5 times with each leg**

◆ **Chin-ups:** These are difficult because they use weaker arm and back muscles. From a hanging position, pull yourself up with your torso straight. Use your arms, without twisting your back. Try to raise yourself until your chest is at or near the bar. Hold for one or two seconds then lower yourself down slowly. **Goal = 3 - 5 times**

◆ **Bottle curls:** Start with two bottles of laundry detergent (or any large bottle with a handle). Stand with your feet flat on the floor, shoulder width apart. Place both your hands in the same position on the handles of each bottle. With your back straight, slowly curl each bottle keeping your arm in the shape of an "L" until the bottle is raised to your shoulder. Only use bottles that you can lift easily and that do not cause you to stumble under their weight. **Goal = 5 times with each arm**

◆ **Heel Raises:** Heel raises strengthen the calf muscles. Stand with your feet a few inches apart, with your hands lightly resting on a counter or chair in front of you. Slowly raise your heels off the floor while keeping your knees straight. Hold for 5 seconds and then slowly lower your heels to the floor. Repeat. **Goal = 8 - 10 times**

◆ **Squats:** Start by placing your hands on your hips and stand with feet about shoulder width apart. Slowly move downward by bending your knees and keeping body straight by sticking out your butt. Squat as far down as you comfortably can, then slowly rise back up until you are standing straight. **Goal = 5 - 8 times**

◆ **Lunges:** Start by standing with your two feet shoulder length apart with your back straight and your arms by your sides. Simply lunge forward on one knee, count to two and then step back to your original position. After two counts lunge forward on your alternate foot. Always make sure that your front knee never goes beyond your toes. Make sure you keep your balance so you do not fall forward or to the side! **Goal = 5 - 7 times with each leg**

◆ **Push-ups (traditional or modified):** Practice getting your body into a straight position required for a pushup, by stiffening your body like a flat board. Get on the floor and rest on both forearms and toes, with your body stiff and straight off the floor. Keep your butt down without letting it droop towards the floor so it is straight with the rest of your body. When you are ready to start, take your forearms off the floor and place your hands where they were. Lower your body straight down until your chest almost touches the floor, and then push back up into your straight position. Keep your head up and look straight ahead. **Goal = 5 - 10 times**

To do a modified push up, get in your straight position and then rest on your knees. When you are ready to start, lower your body straight down while rocking forward on your knees to help take away some of your body weight. Push back up so you are in your original position. This is a great way to start learning push-ups and building your strength.

COACH JAME'S CORNER
Hey kids, Have fun moving and getting fit! More training videos at: SummerFitLearning.com

Coach James!
Summer Fit Learning

- **Crunches:** Start by sitting down on the floor, then bend your knees while moving your feet toward your butt. Keep your back and feet flat on the floor. Put your hands behind your head, or arms together in front of your body with your hands tucked under your chin. With your shoulders off the ground as the starting position, raise your head to your knees, using only core muscles. Then lower your body, keeping your shoulders slightly off the ground in the starting position. Try to keep your lower back on the floor and do not use your arms to pull yourself up. **Goal = 5 - 10 times**

- **Can Do:** Go to the kitchen and find two of the heaviest cans you can hold. Stand with your feet flat on the floor, with the cans in your hands and arms at your side. Lift the cans up to your chest, bending your arms at the elbows. Hold for two seconds, and then slowly lower your arms. **Goal = 3 - 5 times**

- **Sky Reach:** Choose a small object such as a ball, a book or even a piece of fruit. Make an "L" with your arm—with your upper arm at shoulder level and your forearm pointing toward the ceiling. Now extend your arm straight over your shoulder, pushing the object toward the sky. Return to the bent-arm position. **Goal = 3 - 5 times with each arm**

- **Bottle Lift:** Start with two bottles of laundry detergent (or any large bottle with a handle). Stand with your feet flat on the floor, shoulder width apart. Place the bottles on each side of your feet. Bend your knees, grab the bottles and stand up. **Goal = 5 - 10 times**

- **Chop n Squat:** Start with legs wide, bring your feet together, then out wide again, reach down and touch the ground, and pop up. **Goal = 7 - 10 times**

- **Side Step:** Lunge out to your right. Back leg straight, bend the right knee. Slide back and bend the left knee and straighten the right leg. Turn and face the opposite direction and repeat. **Goal = 5 times each direction**

- **Balance:** Balance on one foot. Foot extended low in front of you. Foot extended low in back of you. Foot extended low to the side. **Goal = hold each pose for 15 seconds**

- **Toe Taps:** Start by standing with your two feet shoulder length apart with your back straight and your arms by your sides. While jumping straight up, bring one toe forward to the front and tap while alternating to the opposite foot. Go back and forth between your left and right foot. Find a rhythm and be careful not to lose your balance! **Goal = 7 - 10 times with each Foot**

Summer Fit Tip

The more you workout and play with a partner the more they are likely to stick with it. Find a friend or someone in your family to exercise with everyday.

**Marci and Courtney Crozier
Former Contestants of NBC's
*The Biggest Loser***

Exercise Activities for Kids

Find What You Like

Everybody has different abilities and interests, so take the time to figure out what activities and exercises you like. Try them all: soccer, dance, karate, basketball, and skating are only a few. After you have played a lot of different ones, go back and focus on the ones you like! Create your own ways to be active and combine different activities and sports to put your own twist on things. Talk with your parents or caregiver for ideas and have them help you find and do the activities that you like to do. Playing and exercising is a great way to help you become fit, but remember that the most important thing about playing is that you are having fun!

List of Exercise Activities

Home–Outdoor:

Walking
Ride Bicycle
Swimming
Walk Dog
Golf with whiffle balls outside
Neighborhood walks/Exploring
(in a safe area)
Hula Hooping
Rollerskating/Rollerblading
Skateboarding
Jump rope
Climbing trees
Play in the back yard
Hopscotch
Stretching
Basketball
Yard work
Housecleaning

Home – Indoor:

Dancing
Exercise DVD
Yoga DVD
Home gym equipment
Stretch bands
Free weights
Stretching

With friends or family:

Red Rover
Chinese jump rope
Regular jump rope
Ring around the rosie
Tag/Freeze
Four score
Capture the flag
Dodgeball
Slip n Slide
Wallball
Tug of War
Stretching
Run through a sprinkler
Skipping
Family swim time
Bowling
Basketball
Hiking
Red light, Green light
Kick ball
Four Square
Tennis
Frisbee
Soccer
Jump Rope
Baseball

Turn off TV Go Outside - PLAY!

Public Service Announcement
Brought to you by Summer Fit

Chill out on Screen Time

Screen time is the amount of time spent watching TV, DVDs or going to the movies, playing video games, texting on the phone and using the computer. The more time you spend looking at a screen the less time you are outside riding your bike, walking, swimming or playing soccer with your friends. Try to spend no more than a couple hours a day in front of a screen for activities other than homework and get outside and play!

Health and Wellness Index

Healthy Family Recipes and Snacks

Jay Jacobs
Former Contestant
of NBC's
The Biggest Loser

YOGURT PARFAITS: 01

Prep time: 15 minutes
Cook time: 0
Yield: 4 servings
Good for: all ages, limited kitchen, cooking with kids

Ingredients:
2 cups fresh fruit, at least 2 different kinds (can also be thawed fresh fruit)
1 cup low-fat plain or soy yogurt
4 TBSP 100% fruit spread
1 cup granola or dry cereal

It is important to teach children at a young age about the difference between a snack that is good for you versus a snack that is bad for you. It is equally important to teach your kids about moderation and how to eat until they are full, but not to overeat!

YOGURT PARFAITS: 02

Directions:
Wash and cut fruit into small pieces
In a bowl, mix the yogurt and fruit spread together
Layer each of the four parfaits as follows:
Fruit
Yogurt
Granola (repeat)
Enjoy!
Kids can use a plastic knife to cut soft fruit
Kids can combine and layer ingredients

Tips:
A healthier dessert than ice cream
A healthy part of a quick breakfast

SMOOTHIES: 01

Prep time: 5 minutes
Cook time: 0
Yield: 2 servings
Good for: all ages,
limited kitchen, cooking with kids

Ingredients:
1 cup berries, fresh or frozen
4 ounces vanilla low fat yogurt
½ cup 100% apple juice
1 banana, cut into chunks
4 ice cubes

SMOOTHIES: 02

Directions:
Place apple juice, yogurt, berries, and banana in a blender. Cover and process until smooth

While the blender is running, drop ice cubes into the blender one at a time. Process until smooth

Pour and enjoy!
Kids can cut soft fruit and measure ingredients. They can also choose which foods to include.

Variation:
Add ½ cup of silken tofu or ½ cup of peanut butter for extra protein.

PITA PIZZAS: 01

Prep time: 10 min
Cook time: 5-8 minutes
Yield: 2 servings
Good for: all ages, limited kitchen, cooking with kids

Ingredients:
Whole wheat pita bread or whole wheat round bread
Low-fat (part-skim) mozzarella cheese
Tomato or pizza sauce
A variety of toppings: peppers (green, red, yellow or orange), broccoli, mushrooms, olives, apple, pear, pineapple, onions, tomatoes, etc.

PITA PIZZAS: 02

Directions:
Preheat oven or toaster oven to 425°F
Heat pita bread in warm oven for 1-2 minutes
Assemble the pizzas on a cookie sheet:
Spread the tomato sauce on the pita with room for crust
Sprinkle with cheese
Add toppings
Cook pizzas in the oven for 5-8 minutes, or until cheese is melted
Serve immediately with a simple green salad

Kids in the Kitchen:
Kids can choose their toppings
Little kids can cut soft toppings with a plastic fork

Health and Wellness Vocabulary

In order to teach your children the difference between healthy habits and unhealthy habits it is important to know and understand some of the basic terminology that you may hear in the media and from health experts.

Marci Crozier
Former Contestant of NBC's *The Biggest Loser*

VOCABULARY

Calorie: A unit of measure of the amount of energy supplied by food.

Fat: It is one of the 3 nutrients (protein and carbohydrates are the other 2) that supplies calories to the body.

Protein: Is one of the building blocks of life. The body needs protein to repair and maintain itself. Every cell in the human body contains protein.

Carbohydrates: The main function is to provide energy for the body, especially the brain and nervous system.

Type 1 Diabetes: A disease characterized by high blood glucose (sugar) levels resulting in the destruction of the insulin-producing cells of the pancreas. This type of diabetes was previously called juvenile onset diabetes and insulin-dependent diabetes.

Type 2 Diabetes: A disease characterized by high blood glucose (sugar) levels due to the body's inability to use insulin normally, or to produce insulin. In the past this type of diabetes was called adult-onset diabetes and non-insulin dependent diabetes.

Sedentary lifestyle: A type of lifestyle with no or irregular physical activity. It pertains to a condition of inaction.

BMI: An index that correlates with total body fat content, and is an acceptable measure of body fatness in children and adults. It is calculated by dividing weight in kilograms by the square of height in meters. BMI is one of the leading indicators in determining obesity.

Obesity: Refers to a person's overall body weight and whether it's too high. Overweight is having extra body weight from muscle, bone, fat and/or water. Obesity is having a high amount of extra body fat.

Fiber: This is not an essential nutrient, but it performs several vital functions. A natural laxative, it keeps traffic moving through the intestinal tract and may lower the concentration of cholesterol in the blood.

Nutrient dense foods: Foods that contain relatively high amounts of nutrients compared to their caloric value.

Screen time: The amount of time a person participates in watching or playing something on a screen. The screen could be a television, computer, computer games, and a variety of electronics that interact with people utilizing a screen of various sizes. The American Academy of Pediatrics recommends no screen time before age 2 and no more that 1-2 hours of screen time for children over age 2.

Food label: Information listed inside a square box on prepared food packaging that shows the nutritional value of a product one consumes. It also gives the value shown as a percentage of the daily nutritional values that the Food and Drug Administration (FDA) recommend for a healthy diet.

Serving size: This term is used by the United States Department of Agriculture (USDA) to measure amounts of food. It is a tool for healthy eating.

Fat: is a source of energy. Fats perform many important functions in the body. There are healthy fats and unhealthy fats.

Monounsaturated and polyunsaturated oils: These contain some fatty acids that are HEALTHY. They do not increase the bad cholesterol in the body. Some of the foods in this category include fish, nuts and avocados.

Saturated fat: This "solid" fat increases bad cholesterol which can lead to it building up in the arteries and cause disease, more specifically, heart disease.

Trans fat: This fat is mostly found in processed foods and it contains unhealthy oils (partially hydrogenated). This type of fat has been shown to increase the bad cholesterol in the body and lower the good cholesterol.

Preadolescent: generally is defined as ages 9-11 years of age for girls and 10-12 years for boys.

Middle childhood: generally defines children between the ages of 5 to 10 years of age.

"School age": is another word for middle childhood.

"Tween": a relatively new term for a child between middle childhood and adolescence.

Health and Wellness Child Nutrition

1. Preadolescent ("tweens") and school age children's growth continues at a steady, slow rate until the growth spurt they will experience in adolescence. Children of this age continue to have growth spurts that usually coincide with increased appetite. Parents should not be overly concerned about the variability and intake of their school-age children.

2. The importance of family mealtimes cannot be stressed enough. There is a positive relationship between families who eat together and the overall quality of a child's diet.

3. Continue to have your child's BMI-for-age percentile monitored to screen for over and underweight.

4. In this age group the choices a child makes about his or her food intake are becoming more and more influenced by their peers, the media, coaches, and teachers. These outside influences steadily increase as a child ages and becomes more independent.

5. School plays a key role in promoting healthy nutrition and physical activity, so try to participate in healthy, school-related activities with your child, such as walk to school days and volunteering in the school's garden club.

6. Limited physical activity, along with sedentary activities are major contributing factors to the sharp increase of childhood obesity.

7. Soft drink or soda consumption, which tends to increase as a child ages, is associated with increased empty caloric intake and an overall poorer diet. These soft drinks also are a major contributor to dental caries. Diet sodas have no nutrient value, though they are not high in calories.

8. Complications from overweight and obesity in childhood and adolescence are steadily rising. This is including type 2 diabetes (usually adult onset diabetes) and high cholesterol levels.

9. Those children in the age ranges of middle childhood and preadolescence are strongly encouraged to eat a VARIETY of foods and increase physical activity to 60 minutes every day. Parents should set a good example by being physically active themselves and joining their children in physical activity.

10. Parents with healthy eating behaviors and are physically active on a regular basis are excellent role models for their children.

Healthy Websites

www.myplate.gov

www.readyseteat.com

www.nourishinteractive.com

www.cdph.ca.gov/programs/wicworks

www.cdc.gov
(food safety practices, childhood diabetes and obesity)

www.who.int

www.championsforchange.net

www.nlm.nih.gov/medlineplus

Healthly Lifestyles Start at Home

Staying active and healthy is important because it will have a positive impact on every aspect of your life.

Jay and Jen Jacobs
Former Contestants of NBC's
The Biggest Loser

1 **Lead by example:** Your children will do what they see you do. Eat your fruits and vegetables, go for walks and read a book instead of watching television. Your child will see and naturally engage in these activities themselves.

2 **Limit Screen Time:** The American Academy of Pediatrics recommends no screen time before age 2 and no more that 1-2 hours of screen time for children over age 2. Instead of limiting screen time for just them, try regulating it as a household. Keep a log of technology time, note "Screen Free Zones" like the bedroom and try shutting off all technology at least 1 day a week.

3 **Talk at the Table:** Sitting down with the family for dinner gives everybody an opportunity to reconnect and share experiences with each other. Limit distractions by not taking phone calls during dinner and turning the television off.

4 **Drink More Water (and milk):** Soda and other packaged drinks are expensive and contain a lot of sugar and calories. Set an example by drinking water throughout the day and encourage your children to drink water or milk when they are thirsty. These are natural thirst quenchers that provide the mineral and nutrients young (and old) bodies really need.

5 **Portion Control:** There is nothing wrong with enjoying food, but try to eat less. Use smaller plates so food is not wasted and teach your children to tell the difference between being satisfied and overeating.

6 **Make Time For Family Play:** Instead of sitting down to watch TV together plan an activity as a family. Go for a walk or bike ride, work on the yard together, visit the neighbor as a family. It's a great way to reduce technology, but more importantly a great opportunity to enjoy time together as a family.

SUMMER JOURNAL

Write about your
family vacation.

SUMMER JOURNAL

Write about your favorite
outdoor summer activity
Ex: Camping, swimming or biking.

SUMMER JOURNAL

*Write about your
best summer day.*

SUMMER JOURNAL

Write about one of your favorite things to do at home during the summer.

SUMMER JOURNAL

Write about your best friend

Summer Fit Book Report
Fifth to Sixth Grade

Title: _____

Author: _____

Genre (scary, mystery, adventure, biography): _____

Describe the setting: _____

_____

Protagonist (Main Character): _____

_____

Antagonist (Person who is against the protagonist): _____

_____

Summary of the plot: _____

_____

_____

_____

What was your impression of the book? What did you like and dislike about the book?

_____

_____

Would you recommend this book to a freind? Why or why not?

_____

_____

_____

Pretest
1. B, 2. A, 3. C, 4. B, 5. A, 6. C, 7. D, 8. B, 9. B, 10. C, 11. B, 12. A, 13. D, 14. C, 15. B, 16. A, 17. C, 18. B, 19. A, 20. B, 21. B, 22. A, 23. B, 24. B, 25. B, 26. B, 27. A, 28. A, 29. C, 30. B, 31. D, 32. C, 33. C, 34. C, 35. B, 36. D, 37. C, 38. B, 39. C, 40. A, 41. C, 42. C, 43. B, 44. D, 45. A, 46. C, 47. 6, 6, 10, 12, 14, 48. A, 49. D, 50. D

Week 1 Day 1
1. S, 2. SF, 3. SF, 4. S, 5. S, 6. S, 7. SF, 8. S, 9. SF, 10. S Mixed Practice: 1. 4440, 2. 2484, 3. 1968
4. 5902, 5. 2826, 6. 82, 7. 285, 8. 288, 9. 188, 10. 2308

Week 1 Day 1
1. After the concert, for her performance, 2. before the concert tour, 3. like a bird, about her voice practices, 4. behind the curtain, during the performance, 5. with the principal, 6. in the math class, from mine, 7. behind me, during the concert

Week 1 Day 2
1. C, 2. South Baldwin Co., Foley, Alabama, 3. Answers will vary. 4. 6:00 AM

Week 1 Day 2
1. correl, either or, 2. sub, Whenever, 3. sub, Although, 4. coord, and, 5. correl, both, and, 6. sub, Because, 7. coord, but, 8. correl, whether, or, 9. sub, Unless, 10. correlative, Either

Week 1 Day 3
1. A = 27.5 cm², 2. A = 45 cm², 3. A = 16 cm², 4. A = 4.1 cm²
Figure 1: Answers will vary. Figure 2: Answers will vary.

Week 1 Day 3
1. elements, 2. number, 3. weight, 4. symbol, 5. period, 6. group, properties, 7. similar

Week 1 Day 4
1. Good grief! 2. Oh, dear! 3. Good grief! 4. Hurrah! 5. Oops! 6. Goodness! 7. Oh, my! 8. Help! 9. Ouch! Prohibition Era: 1. To make the sale and distribution of alcohol as a beverage illegal, 2. Increased crime, economic hardship for law enforcement, 3. To legalize sales of alcohol, 4. Improved economic conditions/sales of alcohol and reduce crime.

Week 1 Day 4
1. Sydney Opera House, 2. Mount Rushmore, 3. Grand Canyon, 4. Leaning Tower of Pisa, 5. Great Sphinx, 6. Great Wall of China

Week 1 Day 5
1. 23, 2. 3, 3. debt, 4. unsuccessful, 5. honest

Week 2 Day 1
1. PS, 2. F, 3. PR, 4. F, 5. PR, 6. PS 7. B

Week 2 Day 1
1. 466,783, 2. 1,656,907, 3. 1,252,368, 4. 2,023, 5. 78,994, 6. 76,597,490, 7. 100,111, 8. 290 9. 10 ones were added, increasing the number by 10. 10. 10 tens were added, increasing the number by 100.
11. 10 hundreds were added, increasing the number by 1,000. 12. 10 thousands were added, increasing the number by 10,000, 13. 10 hundreds were added, increasing the number by 1,000.
14. >, 15. <, 16. <, 17. =, 18. >, 19. <

Week 2 Day 2
1. C, 2. A, 3. D, 4. A, 5. B, 6. C, 7. C 8. A, 9. B, 10. A

Week 2 Day 2
1. Going to California was the best vacation I've ever had. 2. "Before we leave this afternoon, be sure to feed the dog," Mom said. 3. Mrs. Martin brought brownies to the party, and she helped us clean up when it was over. 4. "I think it would be fun to travel to London, England one day," said Marcus. 5. Conner's portion of meat includes three pieces of chicken, beef, and fish. 6. "Where are your sandals?" Harriett asked her little sister. 7. The soft, sweet, loving kitten purred as Jennifer picked her up. 8. Yes, thank you, Steve, I will take care of making all of the arrangements.

Week 2 Day 3
1. American Civil War to WWI, 2. WWI 3. poor economy, 4. Great Depression 5. Army, Navy, Air Force, and Marine Corps

Week 2 Day 4
Answers will vary but will result in shorter word count. Entire words will be replaced with letters, numbers, symbols, etc., reflecting current day trends.

Week 2 Day 4
1. Answers will vary. 2. Answers should be in numerical form with label in miles. 3. Answer should be in hours and minutes, labeled. 4. Answer should be 2 names of locations. 5. Answer should be a known landmark or places of interest. 6. Answer should be an overnight stay facility within the route.

Week 2 Day 5
1. how to give injections; how to make hospital beds; care for newborn babies; care for very sick people. 2. cholera or smallpox. 3. She cared for very sick people by working in small village hospitals. 4. She was worried she might hurt them because the babies were so small. 5. Her ability to stay calm during a crisis impressed her colleagues.

Week 3 Day 1
Suggested answers: 1. To state an opinion of bad school food and how to solve it. 2. It was something he/she had strong feelings and opinions and wanted to help solve the problem. 3. From personal experiences, eating food, speaking to friends, the writer had "first hand" knowledge about the topic. 4. Other students' opinions as well as the cafeteria managers were considered.

Week 2 Day 3

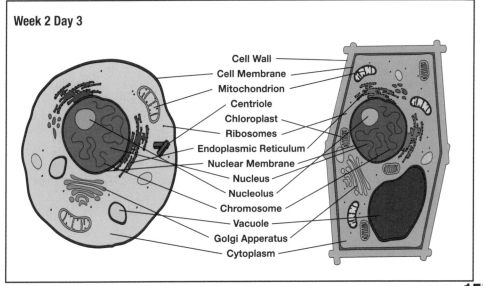

Cell Wall
Cell Membrane
Mitochondrion
Centriole
Chloroplast
Ribosomes
Endoplasmic Reticulum
Nuclear Membrane
Nucleus
Nucleolus
Chromosome
Vacuole
Golgi Apperatus
Cytoplasm

Week 3 Day 1

1. J, 2. C, 3. H, 4. G, 5. A, 6. I, 7. F, 8. B, 9. E, 10. D, 11. 20, 12. 28, 13. 13, 14. 7, 15. 12, 16. 6, 17. 76, 18. 25, 19. 8, 20. 8

Week 3 Day 2

1. Past Perfect, 2. Future Perfect, 3. Present Perfect, 4. Future Perfect
Decimal Number Line: In order from left to right: 3/4, 1 1/2, 1.75, 2, 2 1/4, 2 1/2, 2.75, 3.25, 3.5, 3 3/4

Week 3 Day 2

1. physical, reversible; 2. chemical, irreversible; 3. chemical, irreversible; 4. physical, reversible; 5. physical, reversible; 6. chemical, irreversible; 7. chemical, irreversible.

Week 3 Day 3

1. T, 2. T, 3. F, 4. F, 5. T (Insert grid here and add tree on #1; add star on #2; add smiley face for #3; add ? for #4. See answer key.)

Week 3 Day 3

1. A, 2. D

Week 3 Day 4

1. 30 cm^3 2. 18 cm^3 3. 8 cm^3 4. 60 cm^3
5. 48 cm^3

Week 3 Day 4

1. ascertain, 2. create, 3. encourage, 4. choose, 5. educate, 6. surrender, 7. explain, 8. expose, 9. lively, 10. convict

Week 3 Day 5

1. freedom, 2. Underground Railroad, 3. 300, 4. seven, 5. Moses, 6. South Carolina, 7. justice, duty, 8. nurse, spy, commando

Week 4 Day 1

1. mountains, "float," mountains, 2. oceans, collide, volcanic mountain, 3. mountain range, "protection," oceans, 4. islands, shift, basin, 5. ocean basin, have boundaries, island, 6. weathering slide, weathering, 7. continents, deformable, undersea mountains

Week 4 Day 1

1. G, 2. D, 3. L, 4. K, 5. O, 6. A, 7. I, 8. E, 9. B, 10. C, 11. H, 12. M, 13. J, 14. F, 15. N

Week 4 Day 2

1. B, generous, 2. D, treasures, 3. A, blanket, 4. B, instrument, 5. B, losing, 6. A, excellent, 7. C, threaten, 8. B, information, 9. D, earliest, 10. C, happiness, 11. C, persuasive, 12. B, anniversary, 13. A, obligation, 14. C, submitted, 15. D, considerate

Week 4 Day 2

1. It was for less than the full cost for a buyer because they could get a loan for 80-90% of the price. 2. March 1929, 3. brokers, 4. everyday people, 5. A stock sold on a margin falls below the loan amount, 6. Dow Jones Industrial Average, 7. Black Thursday

Week 4 Day 3

1. 2,968, 2. 2,888, 3. 5,824, 4. 2,585, 5. 5,850, 6. 5,568, 7. 17,240, 8. 20,080 9. 23,408, 10. 38,947, 11. 9,430, 12. 33,374, 13. 22.09, 14. 304.25, 15. 201, 16. 264.53, 17. 231.79, 18. 332.35

Week 4 Day 3

1. sewing machine, 2. Winchester rifle, 3. First Submarine and first digital computer, 4. sewing machine, 5. reaping machine, telegraph, telephone, fan, sewing machine, dishwasher, and zipper. 6. fan and sewing machine.

Week 4 Day 4

Answers will vary due to designing a magazine ad.

Week 4 Day 4

Answers will slightly vary. 1. to have enough money from day to day, 2. when trouble happens, it seems to not just be one thing but many, 3. to work as hard as you possibly can, 4. when two or more people think the same thing, 5. trick or deceive someone, 6. easy to do, 7. to take over looking after another, 8. take on more than one can handle, 9. give away a secret, 10. a person who talks far more aggressively than he/she acts, 11. escaping something at the last minute, 12. doing something too quickly means someone will probably make mistakes and have to do something again. 13. to allow a situation to get out of control, 14. when trouble happens, it seems to not just be one thing but many, 15. someone has given up and stopped trying.

Week 4 Day 5

1. she lettered in basketball, 2. lead her team to win the Gold Medal at the 2008 Beijing Summer Olympics, 3. Answers will vary: 1. lead group of teens to Egypt to paint an orphanage, 2. traveled to the Bahamas to construct a learning center, 3. traveled to Mexico to serve meals to American missionaries, 4. part of a team that created a Hurricane Karina fundraiser in 2005.

Week 5 Day 1

1. D, 2. she did not enjoy teaching, 3. Little House on the Prairie

Week 5 Day 1

1. the cord, 2. Because they have received energy from a battery, etc. and their path is complete, making the flow possible. 3. a path, 4. volts or voltage, 5. provide energy

Week 5 Day 2

1. 14, 2. 16, 3. 5, 4. 14, 5. 25, 6. 19, 7. 9, 8. 50, 9. 6, 10. 127, 11. 10, 12. 14, 13. 36, 14. 14, 15. 98, 16. 14, 17. 9, 18. 68, 19. 84, 20. 5, 21. 14, 22. 10 23. 10, 24. 64, 25. 512, 26. 14, 27. 51 28. 50, 29. 14, 30. 45

Week 5 Day 2

Answers will vary.

Week 5 Day 3

1. hundredths, 2. tenths, 3. thousandths, 4. hundredths, 5. hundredths, 6. tenths, 7. 13.44, 8. 119.7, 9. 3.63, 10. 4.9, 11. 175.85, 12. 7.992, 13. 13.6, 14. 20.713, 15. 11.25, 16. 54.707, 17. 15.9, 18. 21.4, 19. 15.41, 20. 102, 21. .803, 22. .106, 23. 7.013, 24. 4.783, 25. 2.403, 26. 7, 27. 3.403, 28. 1.5, 29. 30, 30. 2.6, 31. 75, 32. 9000, 33. 4.5, 34. 7.0, 35. 500 36. 300, 37. 200.25, 38. 220.8, 39. 600, 40. 60.525, 41. 1,200.4 42. 9.16 43. 10.154, 44. 28.62, 45. 14.6 46. 8.839, 47. 75.92, 48. 3

Week 5 Day 3

1. F, 2. F, 3. T, 4. F, 5. F, 6. T

Week 5 Day 4

1. 4/8 or 1/2, 2. 2/4 or 1/2, 3. 3/8, 4. 12/12 or 1, 5. 7/10, 6. 3/8, 7. 3/5, 8. 7/9, 9. 2/15, 10. 12/16 or 3/4, 11. 7/8, 12. 3/8, 13. 3/8, 14. 7/9, 15. 9/11, 16. 1/16, 17. 2 3/3 or 3, 18. 4 12/8 or 51/2 19. 4, 20. 3, 21. 9 4/3 or 10 1/3, 22. 1 4/8 or 1 1/2, 23. 7 1/3, 24. 4, 25. 1

Week 5 Day 4

1. simile, 2. metaphor, 3. simile, 4. metaphor, 5. simile, 6. metaphor, 7. simile, 8. metaphor, 9. simile, 10. simile

Week 5 Day 5

1. T, 2. T, 3. T, 4. T, 5. T

Week 6 Day 1

1. needed, 2. was, 3. was, 4. correct, 5. correct, 6. was, 7. was, 8. was, 9. marched, 10. followed

Week 6 Day 1

1. 3/8, 2. 7/24, 3. 12/88 or 3/22, 4. 10/90 or 1/9, 5. 6/91, 6. 3/10, 7. 2/5, 8. 1/108, 9. 2/7, 10. 15/32, 11. 2/45, 12. 2/27, 13. 3/4, 14. 3/8, 15. 1 2/3, 16. 4 3/8, 17. 7/12, 5/12

Week 6 Day 2

Today's Blog Update: Answers will vary but should relate to a book and reflect the narrative style of writing. Helpful links: Lists of web resources should be listed as a web address or an entire url. Answers will vary but listed items should include dictionary, thesaurus, book list, web links, etc. This Week's Picture! Answers will vary. Image should be relative to the text on the left and of non-copyrighted stock.

The Joke Corner: Answers will vary. Humor or joke content will be considered.

Week 6 Day 2

3. 377.54, 4. 387.59, 5. 337.72, 6. 322.22, 7. 358.34, 8. 559.32, 9. 504.51, 10. 474.51, 11. 499.51

12. Answers vary 13) Least activity in June; most in August; 14. $416.24

Week 6 Day 3

See crossword answers on page 158

Week 6 Day 3

Ocean Currents: Answers vary

Week 6 Day 4

1. 3/4, 2. 1/5, 3. 1/2, 4. 1/4, 5. 4, 6. 1/7 7. 1 3/4, 8. 1/3, 9. 1/6, 10. 6, 11. 1/6, 12. 2/5, 13. 6 2/3, 14. 4 1/3, 15. 1/20, 16. 2/3, 17. On Tuesday of next week with her dentist, 18. During the press conference, about the many traffic problems, 19. of the softball team, with the club emblem, 20. During the concert at the park, inside the concession area, 21. Under my father's desk, 22. within three months, 23. from Atlanta to Savannah, GA, 24. of food, of lemonade, inside the car, 25. Between 1830 and 1860, about 50,000 slaves to freedom, 26. on her thesis

Week 6 Day 4

1. Anthony can play the drums, or he can play the guitar. 2. Mary Alice pushed the button, and the old bookcase moved. 3. Muhammad Ali was a boxer who never wanted to quit, but Ali has Parkinson's disease. 4. Ginger went to work, but she did not want to go. 5. That movie looks great, and I would love to come see it with you.

Week 6 Day 5

1. Jim Crow, 2. 4, give, 3. seamstress, 4. right, 5. December 20, 1956

Week 7 Day 1

1. C, 2. B, 3. B

Week 7 Day 1

1. F, 2. T, 3. F, 4. T, 5. T, 6. T

Week 7 Day 2

1. 4.37, 2. 2540, 3. 18.64, 4. 1, 5. 50,000, 6. 457.2, 7. 8000, 8. 10, 9. 254, 10. 1.864, 11. 12, 12. 1, 13. 1000, 14. 3.38, 15. .17, 16. 36, 17. 1,563, 18. 1, 19. 72, 20. 321.76, 21. .135, 22. .50, 23. 528.34, 24. 12,000,

Week 7 Day 2

1. past, 2. wear, 3. to, 4. aisle, 5. waste, 6. knew, 7. their, 8. buy, 9. read, 10. road, 11. close, 12. break

Week 7 Day 3

1. Because the legislatures (states) did not vote to approve those. 2. 5, they are: 12, 17, 20, 22, 25, 27. 3. 5 and 6, 4. Answers may vary. Number of terms allowed, limitations of office and secret service. 5. It is more clearly defined by the amendments as they more completely state the topic in the Constitution, but in greater detail.

Week 7 Day 3

1. b, 2. a, 3. a, 4. c, 5. b

Week 7 Day 4

1. claustrophobic, 2. thermostat, 3. bibliography, 4. dermatologist, 5. astronomer, 6. autoimmune, 7. telescope, 8. psychology

Week 7 Day 4

1. Revolution War and Civil War, 2. waste of resources and lives, 3. Great Lakes, Atlantic Ocean, 4. three, 6,000

Week 7 Day 5

1. uncommon, 2. India and Africa, 3. The Father of the Nation, 4. pray, disciplined, honest, possessions, respect, 5. shot

Week 8 Day 1

1. board, therefore, agreed 2. members, you may recall, voted 3. Indeed, 4. is, in fact, extremely 5. always, as a result, treat 6. C 7. D, 8. B, 9. A, 10. B, 11. B

Week 8 Day 1

Answers will vary.

Week 8 Day 2

See crossword answers on page 158

Week 8 Day 2

1. Plants are absolutely not able to grow on R Horizon. 2. Seeds need to germinate on Horizon A where almost no broken rock is found. 3. Studying the soil layers is a way of looking at changes to all soil horizons. 4. Each horizon is most similar to these right above or right below it because of greater similarities. 5. Horizons E, B, and R are most conducive to elevation and minerals and rock deposition.

Week 8 Day 3

1.Their, 2. its, 3. whose, 4. ours, 5. Hers, its 6. yours, 7. Possible answers: 1) $(6 \times 6) + 24 = 60$, 2) $(5^2) + (7 \times 5) = 60$ 3) $6 + 54 = 60$, 4) $100 - 40 = 60$, 8. Possible answers: 1) $7 \times 12 = 84$, 2) $80 + 4 = 84$, 3) $100 - 16 = 84$, 4) $(4^2) + (30 \times 2) + 8 = 84$, 9. Possible answers: 1) $8 \times 4 = 32$, 2) $100 - 68 = 32$, 3) $(2 \times 4) + (8 \times 3) = 32$, 4) $98 - 66 = 32$, 10. Possible answers: 1) $8 \times 7 = 56$, 2) $50 + 6 = 56$, 3) $(4 \times 2) \times (3 + 4) = 56$, 4) $2 (25 - 5) + 16 = 56$

Week 8 Day 3

1. F, 2. K, 3. E, 4. G, 5. D, 6. C, 7. I, 8. J 9.H, 10. A, 11. B

Week 8 Day 4

A. Born in Los Angeles, California
C. Received B.S. Degree in physics
II. Career in space sciences
  2. Astronaut training at NASA
B. Notable career highlights
  2. Mission specialist assignments
  1. Assigned to NASA headquarters
  2. Honors and awards
A. Started Sally Ride Science Company

Week 8 Day 4

1. (-9), 2. (-3), 3. 27, 4. 7, 5. (-18), 6. 20 7. (-1), 8. (-11), 9. 15, 10. (-14), 11. 26, 12. (-27), 13. (-29), 14. (-38), 15. 41, 16. 51, 17. 20, 18. (-29), 19. (-44), 20. (-3), 21. (-47)

Week 8 Day 5

1. False, 2. True, 3. True, 4. False, 5. True

Week 9 Day 1

1. $1/2, 3/4, \sqrt{2}, 1.618, \sqrt{3}, 1\ 3/4$, $2, \sqrt{5}, 2.35, 3.14159$
1. <, 2. <, 3. >, 4. =, 5. <, 6. <, 7. <, 8. < 9. >, 10. >, 11. > 12. <

Week 9 Day 1

Answers/drawing will vary, however, should include 12 items as identified.

Week 9 Day 2

1. S, 2. O, 3. O, 4. O, 5. S, 6. S, 7. O, 8. O, 9. E, 10. H, 11. B, 12. i, 13. F, 14. J, 15. D, 16. G, 17. A, 18. C

Week 9 Day 2

See crossword answers on page 158

Week 9 Day 3
1. (1,3), (2,5), (3,7), (4,9), (5,11)
2. (1,6), (2,11), (3,16), (4,21), (5,26)
3. (1,1), (2,-1), (3,-3), (4,-5), (5,-7)
4. (1,2), (2,5), (3,8), (4,11), (5,14)
Week 9 Day 3
1. 4/10 or 2/5, 2. 17/28

Week 9 Day 4
1. brief, 2. whether, 3. ceiling, 4. dessert
5. past, 6. coarse, 7. neither, 8. copies,
9. advice, 10. heroes, 11. chief, 12. apology,
13. conscious, 14. leisurely, 15. peculiar, 16.
necessary, 17. grabbed, 18. indicate,
19. loneliness, 20. economic, (21-25 possible
answers) 21. The fact that Mrs. Carlson
gave the Red Cross all her money explained
why she declared bankruptcy. 22. The boat
bumped the edge of the dock, but the dock
did not need many repairs. 23. Katy's sister
wondered if Amy was tall enough to be a
model.
Week 9 Day 4
Answers will vary.

Week 9 Day 5
Sequence order should be as follows:
10, 4, 1, 9, 7, 2, 6, 8, 5, 3

Week 10 Day 1
1. C   2. B   3. B   4. C
Week 10 Day 1
1. 96   2. 360

Week 10 Day 2
1. Austria, 2. Portugal, 3. Greece, 4. Poland,
5. Sweden, 6. Bulgaria, 7. Finland, 8. Belgium,
9. Denmark, 10. Italy, 11. France, 12. Norway,
13. Germany, 14. Spain, 15. Iceland,
16. Romania
Week 10 Day 2
Answers will vary. 1. Key ideas: Erosion of
rock, soil by wind, and water are gradual and
sudden. Earth landscapes change by erosion,
usually more gradually so less noticeable.
2. Weathering infers moving particles;
deposition infers stopping and collecting.
3. Items may include personal references
as well as conservation of natural resource
examples. 4. Earth's history of plant and
animal life.

Week 10 Day 3
1. B, 2. A, 3. C, 4. D, 5. C
Week 10 Day 3
Answers to the narrative will vary.

Week 10 Day 4
Answers will vary. Students should have a
wide variety of ideas and answers.
Week 10 Day 4
1. B, 2. C, 3. D, 4. A, 5. B, 6. B, 7. A, 8. B, 9. C,
10. D, 11. A, 12. B, 13. C, 14. C, 15. D

Week 10 Day 5
1. two, 1804 to 1806, 2. Jefferson,
3. Mississippi River to the Pacific Ocean,
4. Corps of Discovery Expedition, 5. 1) discover
new plants and animals, 2) trade with Native
American tribes, 3) make maps and charts of
their course

Week 6 Day 3

Week 8 Day 2

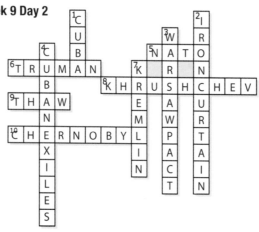

Week 9 Day 2

CONGRATULATIONS!

your name

Has completed
Summer Fit!

and is *ready for Sixth Grade!*

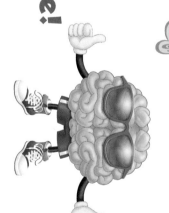

Parent or guardian's signature